all about children

AN INTRODUCTION TO CHILD DEVELOPMENT

Dorothy Baldwin

Oxford University Press

Oxford University Press, Walton Street, Oxford OX2 6DP

Oxford   New York   Toronto
Delhi   Bombay   Calcutta   Madras   Karachi
Kuala Lumpur   Singapore   Hong Kong   Tokyo
Nairobi   Dar es Salaam   Cape Town
Melbourne   Auckland   Madrid

and associated companies in
Berlin   Ibadan

Oxford is a trade mark of Oxford University Press

© Oxford University Press 1983
First published 1983
Reprinted 1983 (twice), 1984, 1985, 1987, 1988, 1991, 1993
ISBN: 0 19 832715 3

Acknowledgements

Illustrations are by Karen Daws, Anna Hancock, Joe Wright and Kathy Wyatt.
The cover illustration is by Tom McArthur.
The cover design is made from Large Pattern Cubes ref N2966H, available from James Galt & Co Ltd.

The publishers would like to thank the following for permission to reproduce photographs:

Department of Medical Illustration, University of Aberdeen, p. 60; Paul Barnard, p. 155 (top); Department of Medical Illustration, St. Bartholomew's Hospital, p. 89 (right); BBC Hulton Picture Library, pp. 14, 179: Camera Press, pp. 85 (right), 136, 155; Department of Medical Illustration, Charing Cross Hospital, p. 41; El Paso Centennial Museum of the University of Texas at El Paso, p. 106; Family Planning Association, p. 35; Ian Fraser, pp 89 (left), 182; Henry Grant, pp. 23, 85 (left), 183, 187; Richard and Sally Greenhill, pp. 7 (inset), 8, 9 (nos. 1–5), 10, 18, 19, 32, 50, 59, 70, 96, 110, 118, 122, 152, 154 (bottom), 171, 172, 175, 180; B.J. Harris Photography, p. 20; Health Education Council, p.47; Heathrow Airport Authority, p. 71; Camilla Jessel, pp. 49, 53, 58, 68, 72, 129, 130 (top), 139, 142, 143, 147, 148, 151, 164; Mansell Collection, p. 7 (bottom); National Children's Home, pp. 9 (no. 6), 188; Photographs and All That, pp. 67, 126, 191; Pictorial Press, p. 140; Department of Medical Illustration, John Radcliffe Hospital, pp. 39, 77, 149, 190; John Rasmussen, p.157; Rolenworth Ltd., p. 91; Medical Illustration Support Service Ltd., Royal College of Surgeons, p. 44; Jeffrey Tabberner, p. 75; Jenny Thomas, pp. 31, 146; World Health Organization, p. 135; The Zoological Society of London, p. 105.

The publishers would like to thank the following examination boards for permission to include questions from examination papers:

East Anglian Examinations Board (EAEB)
East Midland Regional Examinations Board (EMREB)
Oxford Delegacy of Local Examinations (O)
Southern Regional Examinations Board (SREB)
Southern Universities Joint Board (SUJB)
South-Western Examinations Board (SWEB)
West Midlands Examinations Board (WMEB)

The author would like to thank Kenneth David for his help in reading the manuscript.

Photoset by Rowland Phototypesetting Limited, Bury St Edmunds, Suffolk.
Printed by Butler & Tanner Ltd, Frome and London.

Preface

All about children is suitable for pupils working towards GCSE examinations in Home Economics: Child development. The book can also be used by those interested in nursery nursing as a career, and by others who wish to study a straightforward course in early human development without taking any examinations.

The book contains seven chapters, each of which is broken down into a number of self-contained double-page units. Each unit deals with one particular topic in detail and ends with questions designed to reinforce understanding of the main teaching points. Many of the units contain a 'points to consider' section which acts not only as a summary but as a useful tool for discussion and evaluation of the material.

At the end of each chapter is a section of further work. This provides suggestions for learning through direct observation, for practical study, for homework, and for individual project work. Visits to various external agencies are recommended and where this is not possible, alternative suggestions for study are offered. The questions provide a wide variety of extended work from which the teacher may select, according to the needs and abilities of the students. Practice in answering examination questions is also included.

The book is designed to be of real value to the teacher in the classroom, especially those working with groups and those tackling the subject of child development for the first time. Slowly, step by step, the beginnings of human life are built up by careful explanation and by the use of clear, simple language and illustrations. Gradually, more difficult concepts concerning the child's psychological growth and development are introduced. Some of these later units may be passed over by students of lower ability, but the information is presented in such a way as to make the facts readily accessible to all but a few. The language used is self-explanatory and written work can be undertaken unaided while the teacher is engaged in the practical aspects of the course.

Where possible, the word 'parent' has been used throughout the text, except where 'mother' is absolutely essential. Other adult figures such as doctors and social workers are also referred to as 'she'. From the beginning, the child is called a 'he', for the sake of clarity rather than from any sexist inclination.

Contents

Chapter 5: Mental health – development of the mind

Chapter 6: Emotional health – development of the feelings

Chapter 7: Children with special needs

Chapter 1

Changes in family life

The structure of the family

The family is a small group of people, related by kinship (blood or marriage), in which one or more children are cared for by one or more adults within some kind of home.

In most countries, the laws concerning marriage insist on monogamy (one husband, one wife). In some Muslim countries, it is still lawful for one husband to have as many as four wives. This is called polygamy: it is getter much rarer. Polyandry (where wives are allowed to have more than one husband) is now very rare indeed.

Different family structures

Among the Mossi tribe in Upper Volta, West Africa, the eldest sons are sent away to be raised by grandparents until they are twelve or thirteen. Babies must be born in their father's village, but the mothers return to their own villages during the child's first years of life.

On the islands of Samoa in the Pacific, child care is shared by all the women in a village of some forty or fifty households. They can depend on help from a wide variety of uncles, grandfathers, cousins, as well as the father – all of whom have to be respected. There is less closeness between the natural parents and child, but this does not seem to matter as there are so many caring adults around.

In industrialized countries today, the 'average' family is made up of mother, father and about 2.5 children. But there are as many different family structures as there are different kinds of people to fit them.

Look at the photographs on the next page. These show six different family structures:

1   A widowed father with three children.
2   A couple with four adopted children.
3   An unmarried mother and her daughter.
4   A mother, her teenage son, and two foster babies.
5   Grandparents looking after their daughter's baby.
6   A children's home.

You can probably think of many more possible family structures. No one type of family is 'better' than the others.

1   Children can do well or badly in any of these homes.
2   A child needs to feel he is loved, he belongs, he is wanted.
3   He needs to be cared for by people he gets to know and love in return.
4   A child can feel all of these things from any of these different families.
5   A child can feel none of these things from any of these families.
6   The quality (kind) of parenting a child receives is usually far more important than the structure of his family.

Questions

1 Copy out the definition of a family.
2 In your own words, explain the difference between monogamy, polygamy and polyandry.
3 How many people are there in the 'average' family in industralized countries today?
4 In what way does your own family (a) fit in or (b) seem quite different?
5 Copy out the two sentences about what a child needs to do well in any kind of family structure. Learn them.
6 What is meant by 'kinship'? Explain the difference between kinship and friendship.

The shape of the family

Families can be divided into two main groups.

1 The *nuclear* family, which is made up of father, mother, and children living together in the same dwelling.
2 The *extended* family, which may include grandparents, aunts, uncles, and cousins, living together in the same home, or close by in the same neighbourhood.

The nuclear family is more usual nowadays. When a young couple marry, they want to start their new life in a home of their own. The work situation may mean the couple have to leave the neighbourhood – even the country – where the rest of the family live. Grandparents are healthier and live longer. They prefer to stay in their own homes and be independent for as long as possible. Though the nuclear family is more usual, both kinds of family have their advantages and disadvantages.

Left: A nuclear family – a married couple and their children.

Below: An extended family – four generations.

1 Privacy

Living within an extended family can mean less privacy for everyone. The young married couple may think older members are interfering too much in their lives.

Living within a nuclear family means the young couple have all the privacy they want. They can visit older members; they can telephone or keep in touch by letter if they have moved abroad.

2 Company

In an extended family there are so many people coming and going that no one person need feel lonely. Kinship becomes especially important in times of trouble, and as people grow older.

In a nuclear family the couple, especially a new mother, can suffer acute loneliness. Friendship with other couples who have small children becomes very important.

3 Raising children

In an extended family there are plenty of adults to help out with the children. The learning of child care is handed down from generation to generation. In times of stress or illness, the new parents can get all the help and support they need.

In a nuclear family the mother has to cope on her own during the day. Often she has no experience of babies, and this makes her anxious that she is doing the wrong things. In times of trouble she may feel so trapped that she begins to dislike being a mother.

It seems there is a high price to pay for privacy. Also, in the nuclear family, there is a risk that the relationships between parents and children may become too intense. But these risks seem worth taking. Four out of five households in Britain are made up of nuclear family members only. People need privacy, but they need information to cope with the shape of the modern family. There is now a great deal of information about childhood and human behaviour which was not previously known.

Information for the family, whatever its shape

1 Child development is taught in schools and colleges so that everyone can have a better understanding of how the human personality is formed.
2 Antenatal (before birth) clinics give information on child growth and development, as well as looking after the mother and her unborn baby.
3 Support, information, and help are offered to the family by the health visitor and the social worker – people trained in family welfare.
4 Information about love, marriage, sexual relations, and family planning is now available from local health education offices.

Questions

1 **What is meant by the 'nuclear' family?**
2 **What is meant by the 'extended' family?**
3 **Write down three reasons why nuclear families are more common today.**
4 **Write down two disadvantages of living in a nuclear family.**
5 **How many families in Britain are made up of nuclear families? If you live elsewhere, find out the figures for your country and compare them.**
6 **Which would you prefer to live in, a nuclear or an extended family? Write a short essay giving reasons for your answer.**

'The Good Old Days!'

A hundred years ago family life was often difficult, especially for people with little money. In times of hardship, the family was left to struggle alone.

Children

There was a high death rate amongst new-born babies (perinatal mortality), and also for infants in the first two years of life (infant mortality). Many babies were born with some form of mental handicap or physical disability. Babies born outside marriage (illegitimate babies) were likely to be abandoned as 'foundlings'; they were raised in cruelly-run orphanages and charity schools. Children from poor families worked long hours in terrible conditions for very little money in factories started by the Industrial Revolution. As education had to be paid for, many children had little hope of improving their futures.

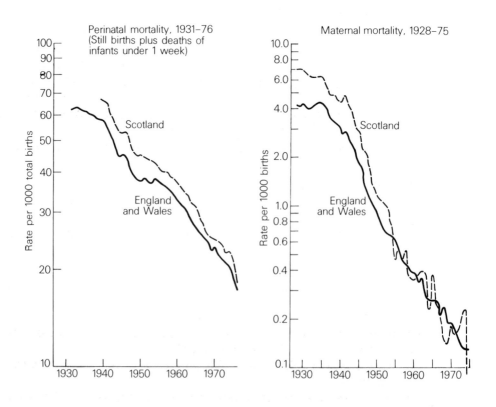

Parents

Mothers died in childbirth from puerperal fever, a disease caused by lack of proper hygiene. As there was no help with family planning, many mothers became ill from too much child-bearing. Poor mothers also had to work hard, which left them little strength to care for their children. The father's lot was not much better – struggling to keep a poorly-paid job while trying to look after his family. Malnutrition (lack of proper diet) was common, and so were diseases caused by lack of hygiene.

Families

Many families managed to be happy in spite of these dreadful social conditions. But some parents gave up the unequal struggle and drowned their miseries in alcohol. Babies were given opiates (sleeping drugs) and sips of gin to quieten their cries of hunger. This damaged their growth.

Women and children had very few legal rights. They were regarded as 'chattels' because they belonged to, and were ruled by, men: husbands, fathers, brothers, uncles, others in authority.

'Gin Lane' by Hogarth.

How long ago were the 'Good Old Days'?

'The whole house was in a bad state of repair and infested by rats. In the four rooms were four adults and fourteen children. Measles broke out among the children, one of them died from pneumonia following it: two were removed to the hospital suffering the same complaint, and one of these also died. A crowning touch of horror was added to the tragedy when the undertaker entering the room with the coffin killed a rat which was trying to get at the dead body of the child . . .
This is not a story of the Middle Ages or of some Asiatic village, but of South London in the year of Our Lord, 1930.'

1 We must be careful not to think too fondly of the 'Good Old Days'.
2 People sometimes do, when they worry over what is going wrong now.
3 Each age seems to bring its own particular problems for the family.
4 When the struggles for survival are removed, other, different hardships have a chance to show through.

Questions

1 **Perinatal mortality means the death of a baby one week before or after birth. What does 'infant mortality' mean?**
2 **What does 'illegitimate' mean? Why do you think the babies were called 'foundlings'?**
3 **Children were regarded as cheap labour by factory owners. From the text, copy out the sentence which shows this to be true.**
4 **Why did some children have little hope of improving their futures?**
5 **Give two reasons why mothers were often too weak to care for their children.**
6 **Write a short essay, explaining why family life was difficult in the 'Good Old Days'.**

New laws for family life

In olden days, marriage often had more to do with legal contracts, money settlements and the legitimacy of children than it had to do with love. We tend to think of medieval times as very romantic, with chivalrous knights wooing fair young maidens with courtly love. But it was not often like that. The following was written by the historian, G. M. Trevelyan, about marriage in the fifteenth century:

> 'The Pastons and other county families regarded the marriages of their children as useful to buy money and estates. If the victims destined for the altar resisted, rebellion was crushed . . . with physical brutality almost incredible. Elizabeth Paston, when she hesitated to marry a battered and ugly widower of fifty, was for nearly three months on end "beaten once in the week or twice, sometimes twice in one day, and her head broken in two or three places". Many parents seem to have cared very little who married their children, provided they themselves got the money.'

As late as the eighteenth century, the following comment was made by the rich young Duke of Kingston:

> '. . . that if he ever married it shall be to have a woman to breed out of and not for a companion . . .'

Changes in attitude to marriage and the family

Possibly the most important changes happened in this century when (a) women were emancipated in 1918 and (b) various education acts were passed leading up to 1944. Once women were free and all children received compulsory education, other rights and freedoms were bound to follow rapidly. From the 1960s onwards, a whole series of new laws has been passed concerned with improving the quality of life for each member of the family. The most major changes are summarized below. They apply, in various forms, to all the industrialized countries.

Major reforms in the law

1 That provision is made for the needs of each member of the family.
2 That family planning should be available so people are free to choose if and when they become parents, and how many children they will have.
3 That under certain circumstances a woman may terminate (stop) an unwanted pregnancy by having an abortion.
4 That when a marriage has 'irretrievably' broken down, the couple may divorce without one partner proving the other guilty of offence (breaking the marriage vows).
5 That incompatability (being extremely unsuited) is sufficient grounds for divorce after a short separation, or after a longer separation if one partner does not want a divorce.
6 That women and children can no longer be evicted (thrown out) from the family home if the man decides to leave.
7 That parents have more than rights over their children: they have duties towards them which they must fulfil.
8 That if parents do not fulfil these duties, their children may be taken from them and put in a safe place of care.

These laws are called 'liberal', which means enlightened, or set free. Some people believe they have destroyed the permanence of the family, while others believe they help to make the family a healthier, happier institution.

The status of women and children has greatly improved. They now have clearly defined rights within the family. Unhappy partners can free themselves from an incompatible relationship without too much legal turmoil. People now expect far more from their marriages in terms of personal fulfilment and happiness than they used to. It may be that the greatest single drawback of these liberating laws is that some children lose the safety of having two loving parents and a secure stable home.

Questions

1 **What was marriage in medieval times often concerned with?**
2 **What happened to Elizabeth Paston when she resisted marriage?**
3 **Look up the word 'irretrievable'. Explain in your own words what is meant by a marriage which has irretrievably broken down.**
4 **Write down which of the new laws for family life you think have improved the status of women.**
5 **Copy out the new laws concerned with the welfare of children.**
6 **Write down the grounds for divorce in the UK. If you live elsewhere, find out what the grounds are in your own country.**

Divorce and family breakdown

Divorce 1966–80 (England and Wales)

Thousands
150 140 130 120 110 100 90 80 70 60 50 40
1966 1967 1968 1969 1970 1971 1972 1973 1974 1975 1976 1977 1978 1979 1980

Number of children under 16 affected by divorce (England and Wales)			
Age of children	1975	1976	1977
0 to 4	33,000	34,000	34,000
5 to 10	69,000	71,000	69,000
11 to 16	43,000	47,000	46,000
Total up to 16	145,000	152,000	149,000

In England and Wales, the Divorce Law Reform Act was passed in 1969, and made complete in 1973. Since then, the number of people getting divorced has risen steadily each year. This trend towards more divorce is common to all industrialized countries. Rising divorce means rising numbers of children at risk of losing one parent and a secure stable home. If the trend towards more divorce continues, a child born today has a 1 in 3.5 chance of being raised in a broken home.

Remarriage

The number of divorced people who remarry has also risen. In fact, thirty per cent of all marriages are remarriages. This means that many children live in new families with only one of their natural parents.

The single parent family

Of the 750,000 single parent families, about three-quarters live alone with no other adult. Fifty per cent more single mothers go out to work than do married mothers who are not divorced. This puts terrible burdens on the mother who may not have the time or energy to care for her children. Sadly, some single mothers do break down. The children are put into the care of local authorities. Some of them lose both parents, though many go back home when their mothers recover.

It is estimated that £5,000,000 is paid each week in supplementary benefits to single parent families who have no other means of support. This money is to help keep families together and not, as a few people suspect, to encourage greed and laziness among single parents – the cost of keeping a child in care is much higher than that of keeping a child at home. But the overriding concern is the child's need to be with his parents. It is the child's safety and happiness which is the most important factor to consider in family breakdown.

One-parent families			
Type	1971	1976	% living alone with children
Divorced mothers	120,000	230,000	76
Separated mothers	170,000	185,000	80
Widows	120,000	115,000	88
Unmarried mothers	90,000	130,000	44
Lone fathers	70,000	90,000	74
Total	570,000	750,000	
Children affected	1 million	1.25 million	

Points to consider

1 These figures may seem shocking: the family may appear to be a very unstable (unsafe) institution for small children.
2 It is important to understand that children can, and do, survive family breakdown as long as they are loved and cared for by both parents.
3 The absent parent needs to keep close ties with the child, otherwise the child will suffer painful feelings of rejection and neglect.
4 Couples should go to marriage guidance counsellors, their local minister, any person whose judgement is respected, for help in sorting out problems long before the relationship reaches the point of family breakdown.

Questions

1 **Write down what rising divorce means to a child born today.**
2 **What sentence shows that divorced people remarry? Copy it out.**
3 **In your own words, explain what sometimes happens when single mothers go out to work.**
4 **What is the real importance of the money paid to single parent families?**
5 **Name two sources of help for a couple who are unhappy. When should they go?**
6 **What most helps children to survive family breakdown?**

The family under attack

Sometimes people attack the whole idea of family life. Some of the more recent attacks are summarized as follows:

1 The family is the source of all human misery.
2 People will never be free until family life is done away with completely.
3 The family is so strong that it stands in the way of progress.
4 The family is so weak that it will soon die out.
5 The growing number of divorces show that people no longer want family life.

There is nothing new about attacks on the family. Throughout history, it has been attacked from many different points of view. These attacks need to be thought about very carefully. Usually they are made by quite small groups of people.

After the Russian Revolution in 1917, the new governments tried to do away with the family completely. Laws were passed which set people free to live as they chose. In his book 'Mother Russia', Maurice Hindus tells us what happened:

> 'Yet the family remained. Its roots were never shaken and were never in danger of being torn out. Despite easy divorce, the right to free and frequent abortions, the overwhelming mass of Russian humanity . . . fell in love, married . . . and stayed married. They raised children. They built a home in the best way they could. Stripped of the compulsions that their grandfathers had known, they chose of their own accord to continue family life . . .'

Alternative family life-styles

People who are not satisfied with family life today try to find different or alternative ways in which to live.

1 *The commune*
This is often made up of people who are not married. Some already have children; some do not. Their hopes are the same as the hopes of the group family – a mutual sharing of all the things which make up family life.

Helping to cook dinner in a commune.

2   *The group family*
This is often made up of members from families which have broken down. The parent left alone with children joins up with others in the same situation. They hope to share love, companionship, work, responsibilities, and equal care for the children in the group.

3   *The kibbutz family*

Children taking their pyjamas to the laundry at Kerem Shalom kibbutz.

Kibbutzim are small farming communities in Israel, with any number from 60 to 2,000 members. During the day, most parents work in the fields; a few stay at home to care for the children and look after the running of the kibbutz. Property belongs to the group; meals are eaten in communal dining rooms; children are cared for in their own communal quarters by special staff. After work, parents and children spend their free time together. At night, children return to their communal sleeping house.

So far, it seems as if only the kibbutzim families are successful. This may be due to much careful planning, immense hard work, and the strength of their passionate devotion to their shared hopes and dreams. The other two groups do not last: they break up after a while and the families go their separate ways.

Questions

1   **Look again at some of the attacks on the family. Do you think people who say these things were likely to have been raised in happy, or unhappy, families? Give reasons for your answer.**
2   **In your own words, write down what happened when the new Russian governments tried to do away with the family.**
3   **Do you think this extract shows that most people want to marry and raise a family? Explain why in your answer.**
4   **What is meant by the 'group family'?**
5   **What is meant by the 'commune'?**
6   **Give reasons why you think the kibbutzim families are more successful than the other alternative life-styles.**

The popularity of marriage and the family

The recent changes in the law, the attacks on the family and the rising number of divorces have not stopped people getting married and raising their families. Nowadays, people are marrying at a much younger age than before. In Great Britain, the average age for marrying in 1911 was 27 for men, and 25 for women; in 1980 it was 23.6 for men and 21.5 for women. People who divorce nearly always hope to marry again. The proportion of the population who are, or have been, married rose from about 52% in 1939 to 62% in 1976. There can be little doubt that marriage is becoming more and more popular.

'Before you are joined in matrimony, I have to remind you of the solemn and binding character of the vows you are about to make.
Marriage is the union of one man and one woman voluntarily entered into for life to the exclusion of all others.'

Marriage is now seen as an equal relationship between the two partners based on love and compatability. This relationship includes:

1 Mutual support in times of trouble and distress.
2 The satisfaction of the sexual needs of the couple.
3 An equal sharing of the work and the responsibilities.
4 Personal freedom <u>within</u> the vows of marriage.
5 Tender loving care by both parents in the upbringing of the children.
6 The provision of a secure stable home for all the members of the family.
7 An equal sharing of the decisions for the good of the family.

Why are there still unhappy families?

1 People marry without enough thought and preparation. They imagine the dream of romantic love will stay at a high peak for ever.

2 People want the dream of family life, but not the hard work or the responsibilities.
3 People marry for the wrong reasons: to 'get' instead of to 'give'.
4 People do not know enough about the needs of children; they dream of cute smiling babies who will be no bother at all.
5 People are people. They can be demanding and difficult.

'You made your bed, now lie on it'

This attitude is no longer held towards unhappy marriages. It seems spiteful, and does not help the family sort out its problems. The more personal fulfilment expected from marriage, the more each of the partners has to work hard at understanding the relationship.

'We have found no better way to raise a child than to reinforce (strengthen) *the ability of his parents, whether natural or substitute, to do so.'*
The Court Report 1976

'Families are and will continue to be the first line of support for children. We have examined other alternatives to the family, and we didn't find any that we thought workable in our society.'
The Carnegie Council on Children 1977

The family and the community

1 The health and welfare of the community depend on the health and welfare of the family.
2 The health and happiness of children depends on the health and happiness of the family.
3 Social factors such as poor housing, lack of money and unemployment do not necessarily cause a happy family to break down.
4 But they add greatly to the misery of families struggling with personal problems. Sometimes, the strain is too great.
5 If we hope for a healthy happy community, a great deal more needs to be done for the welfare of the family.
6 We have come a long way from the 'Good Old Days', but there is still much further we need to go.

Questions

1 **Is marriage getting more, or less, popular than before? Give at least two reasons for your answer.**
2 **Copy out the average age for marrying in 1911 and in 1976. If you live elsewhere, find out the average ages in your country.**
3 **Find out what is meant by 'mutual support'. Write down why you think this is important in marriage.**
4 **What is meant by a 'stable' home? Write one sentence which shows you understand the meaning.**
5 **Write down two reasons why there are still unhappy families.**
6 **What does the health and welfare of the community depend upon?**

Further work on Chapter 1

1 Find out as much as you can about (a) orphanages, (b) charity schools, (c) child labour, in the nineteenth century.

2 Discuss the reasons why you might not have enjoyed being an eight-year-old in the nineteenth century.

3 Do a project on one of the following:
(a) Puerperal fever in childbirth – Joseph Lister and sterilization.
(b) Improved sanitation – John Snow and the water pump.
(c) The emancipation of women – Emily Pankhurst and the suffragettes.

4 Visit your local library and do a project on family life in your own area in the 'Good Old Days'.

5 Find out exactly what is meant by (a) a common-law wife, (b) a co-habitee.

6 From your own observations, describe any family which is different in structure or shape from the average.

7 Discuss the advantages and disadvantages of (a) the nuclear family and (b) the extended family.

8 Find out where the Marriage Guidance office in your area is. If possible, visit them and write an account of their work.

9 Have a class discussion on the attacks on the family.

10 Find out all you can about life on a kibbutz in Israel. Write an account of the way the children spend their day.

11 Some young people find the idea of living in a commune very attractive. Would you? Give reasons for your answer.

12 Discuss the reasons why marriage and the family are so popular. Do you think young people's hopes have changed much over the centuries?

13 Write a short essay on the way marriage is now regarded as compared with the sad tale of Elizabeth Paston (p. 14).

14 A recent study found that married people are, on average, happier than single, divorced, or widowed people. Can you think of reasons for this?

15 Discuss why the people who make up a society must be concerned with the welfare of the family in the community.

16 Do you consider that a large family or a small family could be a better training ground for a young child?
Discuss the advantages and disadvantages of each, with reference to their social and economic status.   (SUJB)

17 (a) What kinds of problems may arise when a step-parent becomes part of an existing family? Suggest ways of overcoming such difficulties.
(b) Many families live in large blocks of flats these days. What are the advantages and disadvantages of this type of home for a young family?   (SREB)

18 Compare the family life of an extended family in a village community with a nuclear family in an urban city area.
What community facilities would be needed by the urban family to replace the help which might be available within the extended family?   (SUJB)

Chapter 2

Developing into an adult

◄ Jennie at 7.

▼ Jennie at 17.

The teen years; the in-between years.
No longer a child, not yet an adult.

Puberty

Puberty is the time when a child's body develops into a young adult's. On average, it starts around 12+ for girls, 14+ for boys. It can start earlier or later: people have their <u>own set time</u> for development which is <u>right</u> for them.

In both sexes, puberty is controlled by special sex hormones. These are important chemicals which travel in the blood. By the end of puberty, the reproductive (sex) organs are working. This means the person is capable of starting a family.

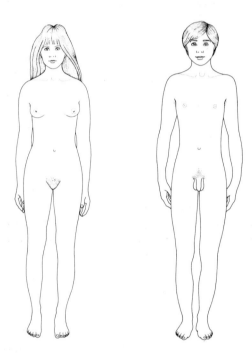

Boys

1 A sudden increase in height called the growth spurt.
2 Increase in size of heart and lungs. Widening of the chest and back.
3 Under-arm hair. Hair around the sex organs (pubic hair).
4 Thick or sparse body hair, depending on family likeness.
5 Facial hair, usually sparse at the beginning.
6 The skin thickens: new sebaceous (oil) and sweat glands start working.
7 The larynx (voice-box) grows larger; the voice breaks, then deepens.
8 Muscles enlarge. The whole body becomes stronger.
9 The penis and testicles grow much larger in size.
10 Sperms (male sex cells) are made in the testicles.

Girls

1 The growth spurt.
2 Increase in size of heart and lungs; widening of the hips.
3 Under-arm hair. Pubic hair above and covering the sex organs.

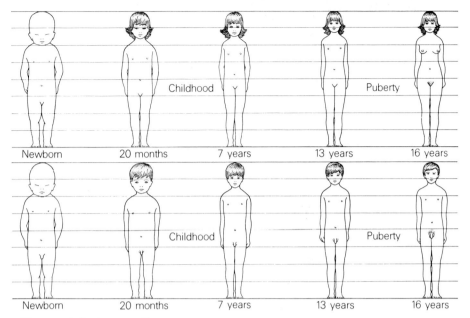

Changes in body proportions.

4 Maybe slight body hair, depending on family likeness.
5 Breasts develop early; may grow larger later on.
6 The skin thickens: new sebaceous and sweat glands start working.
7 A thin layer of fat cells spread under the surface of the skin.
8 Menstruation (periods, monthlies) begin.
9 Eggs (female sex cells) are made in the ovaries.
10 An egg is shed each month during periods, or menstruation (see pp. 28–9).

Worry?

The changes at puberty happen at different times for different people. It is the whole body which develops from a child's to a young adult's. People sometimes worry that they are developing too quickly, or too slowly. There is no need to worry: the changes at puberty can happen in any order and at any time during the teens. However, if not <u>one</u> of the body changes has started by the age of 16, it might be wise to go to the doctor for a check-up.

Questions

1 **What is meant by 'puberty'?**
2 **What is the name of the chemicals which control puberty?**
3 **What is a person capable of once puberty is over?**
4 **There is no average age for puberty to finish. But what is the average age for it to begin in (a) boys and (b) girls?**
5 **Compare the two lists of body changes. Write down the changes which are the same in both sexes. Then write down the changes which happen to the opposite sex only.**

The reproductive organs: boys

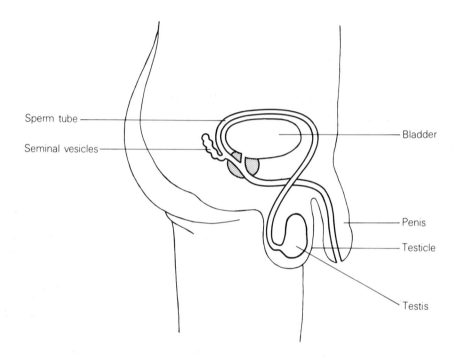

Sperm tube
Seminal vesicles
Bladder
Penis
Testicle
Testis

1 The testicles hang between the legs rather like a pouch.
2 Inside are two testes, one slightly lower than the other.
3 From puberty till old age the testes make sperms (spermatozoa).
4 The testes also make the male sex hormone, testosterone.
5 The sperms travel up a narrow tube and pass glands called seminal vesicles.
6 These glands pour nourishing fluid onto the sperms.
7 The mixture of sperms and nourishing fluid is called semen.
8 The semen travels down the penis and out of the body.
9 The penis is soft as it is made inside rather like a sponge.
10 During sexual excitement it fills up with blood and body fluids.
11 The penis gets firm and hard, and stands away from the body.
12 This is called having an erection.

Questions

1 **Draw and label the male reproductive organs.**
2 **Name the functions of the testes.**
3 **For how long in a man's life is he fertile (able to make sperms)?**
4 **What is the function of the seminal vesicles?**
5 **What is the correct name of the fluid when it has passed the seminal vesicles?**

The reproductive organs: girls

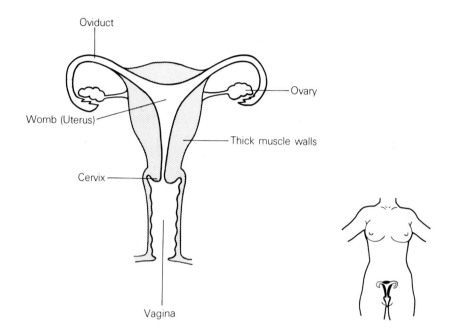

1 The ovaries produce eggs (ova), usually only one each month.
2 They also make and control the female sex hormones, oestrogen and progesterone.
3 The egg is drawn into the fringed 'fingers' at the end of the oviduct.
4 This is a narrow tube which leads from the ovary to the womb.
5 It takes a few days for the egg to be pushed along the oviduct.
6 The womb (uterus) is small, no bigger than the girl's fist.
7 It is made of strong walls of muscle with a narrow space inside.
8 This narrow place is lined with rich layers of blood vessels.
9 They swell and thicken each month to prepare for a 'baby'.
10 The cervix is a closed area of muscle at the neck of the womb.
11 It has a tiny opening for period blood to pass out and sperms to pass in.
12 The vagina is a stretchy tube which leads to the outside of the body.
13 It can stretch to fit a man's penis; it stretches to allow the baby to be born.

Questions

1 **Draw and label the female reproductive organs.**
2 **Name the functions of the ovaries.**
3 **What is the name of the tubes which lead from the ovaries to the womb?**
4 **What is the correct name for the womb?**
5 **What is the name of the muscle at the neck (bottom) of the womb?**

Menstruation

Menstruation is monthly bleeding from the uterus. The blood comes from the rich lining which builds up to prepare for a 'baby'. When there is no baby on the way, the lining breaks down and is shed from the body. This happens each month from puberty onwards. Menstruation is often called a period, or the 'monthlies'.

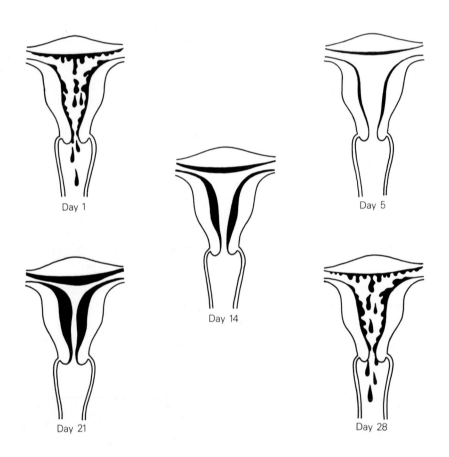

Day 1

Day 5

Day 14

Day 21

Day 28

The uterus (womb)

Day 1   Period begins
Day 5   Period ends
Day 14   Lining is getting thicker
Day 21   Lining ready for 'baby'
Day 28   Unused lining has broken down

The ovary

Egg starts to ripen
Egg still ripening
Egg is released (ovulation)
Egg travels to uterus

Once the period is over, the monthly cycle starts again. The average cycle is 28 days, but it can be any time between 22 and 35 days. At first, menstruation may not happen regularly. There may be one period which is followed by a two or three month gap. It can take up to three years before there is a regular pattern. A few girls are always irregular which makes things a bit difficult – especially when it comes to family planning (p. 36).

Period problems

Menstruation usually begins <u>before</u> ovulation: the womb gets ready for a baby before the first eggs are released. It is thought this is the reason for irregular periods <u>and</u> why there are no uncomfortable period problems early in puberty. However, this does not always apply, as some girls do begin ovulation early, and many girls never have discomfort with periods.

Premenstrual tension (PMT)

This is a feeling of general body tension and slight irritation a few days before the period is due. More water is stored in the body than usual. This causes a few unlucky people to feel bloated and puffy; they may have headaches or sore breasts, they may feel bad-tempered or moody. Cutting down on salt in the diet helps get rid of extra water. Premenstrual tension is unlikely to start before the late teens or early twenties. The discomfort stops as soon as the period starts.

Period pain

The medical name for period pain is dysmenorrhoea. The uterus sheds its lining by muscle contraction, and this causes the 'cramps'. About a third of girls have some period pain, but not before the mid to late teens. In a few girls, the pain can be so bad they feel sick and dizzy too. Taking two aspirin and lying down helps with the immediate miseries. Exercises which act on the muscles around the uterus are needed for a long-term cure.

A woman's fertile life

1   Very early pregnancy, 13+, is not wise because the first eggs may not be fully ripened, and the baby may be born with some kind of disability (pp. 178–9).
2   In late pregnancy, 40+, there is a chance the egg itself may be too old and the baby born with some kind of disability.
3   A girl is fertile from the time of her first ovulation, until she reaches the menopause (the change of life), after which she cannot have a baby.
4   The female sex hormones slow down so that ovulation and menstruation stop.
5   The average age for the menopause is between 45 and 50. Women often look forward to the end of their fertile life, as it releases them from the worries of family planning.

Questions

1   **What is the correct name for a period?**
2   **In your own words, describe what happens at menstruation.**
3   **What is meant by 'ovulation'?**
4   **Name the two different kinds of period problems.**
5   **For how long in a woman's life is she fertile?**
6   **In your own words, explain what happens at the menopause.**

Adolescence

Adolescence is the time of a growth spurt in the <u>mind</u>. This means the emotions and intellect develop; they grow away from the small world of the child. There are many questions to be asked; a great deal of wondering about the future. Adolescence usually starts rather later than puberty.

Some problems

Most people grow through puberty and adolescence very smoothly. But some find there are times of nervous tension and confusion. The changes in the body shape may cause secret worries. The growth spurt in the mind may start up doubts, and lead to conflicts with authority. The newly-working hormones may cause upsets, such as acne, sudden sweating, attacks of shyness, or feeling moody or aggressive.

Remember:
1 Any sudden growth is likely to cause a change.
2 There is no need to get upset; things will settle down.
3 If upsets do start, talk to an older person.
4 Otherwise, relax. The teens are a very happy time.

Hygiene

Extra care is needed with hygiene in the teens, because:
the sebaceous glands make oil to keep the skin and hair healthy;
the newly-working sweat glands leave a grime over the body;
nervous sweating clings to palms of hands, feet, and under-arm hair.

1 If possible, bath every day. If not, a stand-up wash at the sink is essential, making sure the reproductive organs are really clean.
2 It does not take long to rinse through underwear and socks/stockings. Do this each night if there is not a fresh set to wear the next day.
3 Hair should be washed when it begins to look a bit greasy. Brush and comb should be washed at the same time.
4 The face should be washed gently but thoroughly at least twice a day to prevent acne. Try not to pick spots. Dab them with surgical spirit.
5 Before leaving the bathroom, make sure there are no forgotten areas: teeth, ears, nose, and nails all need attention.

The sex drive

1 This is a strong primitive urge to make sure more babies are born.
2 At first, especially in boys, it does not have much to do with love.
3 During puberty most boys have lots of erections.
4 They can happen at any time, but more often happen at night.
5 While asleep or dozing, the semen may be shot out of the penis.
6 This is called nocturnal emission (having a wet-dream).

Coming of age

The physical urge to mate (the sex drive) starts in some people long before they are ready for love and marriage. The emotions and the intellect are slower to develop; they need time to catch up. The average age for this 'catching-up' is put at 18 in many countries.

Young people are advised not to rush into early relationships because of the time difference between puberty and adolescence. Falling in love at 16 may turn out to be a passing fancy, a crush. At 18, people reach their majority in Britain. They come of age; they can marry without their parents' consent.

Questions

1 **What is meant by 'adolescence'?**
2 **Does adolescence start earlier or later than puberty?**
3 **In your own words, explain the difference between puberty and adolescence.**
4 **Name two upsets which can happen during the teens.**
5 **Write down three reasons why extra care must be taken with hygiene during the teens.**
6 **What is meant by the 'sex drive'?**
7 **Do you think that the age of majority is too young, too old, or just about right? Give reasons for your answer.**

Romantic love

*'Love seeketh not itself to please
Nor for itself hath any care
But for another gives its ease
And builds a Heaven in Hell's Despair.'*

For most people, Hell's Despair is being unloved by anyone and overwhelmed with feelings of loneliness. No young person sees his future as being truly alone. Even those who do not want to marry hope to make close loving friends.

Patterns of love

Some people find it hard to imagine their parents were once romantically in love. But they almost certainly were. After marriage, romantic love moves forward to mature affection, which is why parents may be seen as good companions. Sadly, in a few homes, they may seem more like enemies than friends. Young people often make the same kind of marriage as their parents did. Patterns of love are carried on from generation to generation, whether happy or sad. Rushing into an early marriage to get away from parents usually means starting up the same patterns of unhappiness again.

Courtship

This is an old-fashioned word, but the state of courtship still exists. It is an extremely important time for lovers, giving them the chance to find out about themselves and whether they are really compatible (suited or well-matched). People are at their best when courting. They hide away their less attractive side as much as possible, so it is better to break off a relationship if there are many things which do not match. Heartbreak in the late teens is dreadful, but far better than years of misery later on. Courtship is the time for romantic love to move forward to real companionship.

Sexual love

William Blake's beautiful poem is all about 'giving'. He writes that Love puts another's happiness before its own.

Until recently, in all but a few countries, sexual relationships before marriage were forbidden. Young lovers were not allowed to be alone together. Attitudes have changed, but it is still true that most girls and many men are not happy in a sexual relationship where there is no romantic love. Sexual love is like all loving in that it is about 'giving' rather than 'getting'. A man cannot 'give' pleasure if his partner is unhappy and wants to wait until marriage.

Points to consider

1 The older the couple are when they marry, the more chance there is of the marriage being successful.
2 One in three marriages break down when people marry under 20, or where there is a baby on the way.

3 People do not always marry for love; they marry to have a home of their own, to be like everyone else, to feel secure.
4 Marriage is not suitable for everyone. People are different and have different needs. There is nothing 'wrong' in staying single.

Present-day attitudes to marriage

(Totals in both tables exceed 100 per cent because more than one answer could be given.)

What do you think tends to make for a happy marriage? *(Figures are percentages)*

	Total	Men	Women
Comradeship, doing things together	29	27	30
Give-and-take, consideration	28	24	31
Discussing things, understanding	28	26	30
Mutual trust, mutual help, no secrets	20	21	19
Love, affection	19	20	18
Children	14	17	11
Shared interests	13	13	14
Sexual compatibility	5	7	3
Financial security – no debts	5	7	4
Happy home life	5	7	3
Good temper, humour	4	3	4
Home of one's own	1	1	0

What do you think tends to wreck a marriage? *(Figures are percentages)*

	Total	Men	Women
Neglect, bad communication, spouse going out	30	26	33
Selfishness, no give-and-take, intolerance	25	25	25
Infidelity, jealousy	25	29	22
Poverty, extravagance, money disagreements, wives working	17	15	19
Conflicting personalities, no common interests	12	13	12
Temper, arguing, quarrelling, fighting	10	11	9
Sexual incompatibility, fear of more children, no children	10	11	9
Lack of affection, love, general irritation	7	7	8
Drunkenness	7	7	7
Lack of trust, untruthfulness	6	6	7
No house of one's own, bad management, in-laws	4	5	4

Questions

1 **Write down your own favourite poem or words from a song which describes romantic love.**
2 **Give three reasons why courtship is considered an important time.**
3 **Can you think of any reasons why marriage between older couples tends to be more successful than marriage between couples under 20?**
4 **Study the chart, then fill in your own responses to the questions.**

Family planning

Year of marriage	Average family size
1860	6.16
1900	3.3
1910	2.95
1920	2.47
1929	2.08
1980	2.3

Family planning is also called 'contraception' and 'birth control'. There is a well-known joke about family planning: 'try abstinence', which means not having sexual intercourse at all. In countries like China, where the birth rate is increasing to alarming numbers, governments encourage parents to limit their families to one child only. But in Germany during the Second World War, mothers who produced large families were given medals because they were of such service to the State! It is not at all unusual for governments to persuade people to have more or less children according to the needs of the country.

Decisions on family planning

Individual couples have their own ideas about
- (a) if they want children
- (b) when they want children
- (c) how many children they want.

These decisions depend on many different factors both people need to take into account: money, housing, work, as well as the emotional and social needs of the would-be parents.

The decisions on love-making, family planning, and when to start a family are taken jointly by both partners. Nowadays, men do not automatically expect the woman to be totally responsible, though it must be remembered that it is she who is likely to be the more involved, especially in the early years of the child's life.

Advantages of family planning

A baby has a better start in life with:
1 Parents who are not so young that they feel trapped before they have had a chance to grow up themselves.
2 Parents who have been married long enough to be used to each other's different ways.
3 Parents who have a home ready for the baby and are not afraid of the extra expense.
4 Parents who know a baby is hard work and a serious responsibility, as well as being all the fun and joy too.
5 Parents who are ready to settle down to family life.

6 Parents who understand a baby's needs and are prepared to fulfil them.
7 Parents who are happily married and long for a baby.
8 Parents who know a baby will cause a big upheaval in their own feelings.

Lack of planning can lead to:
1 Hasty marriages where the couple may not be suited.
2 Unwanted babies who are rejected by their parents.
3 Single mothers who feel very lonely and unhappy.
4 Abortion, for married women as well as single women.
5 Children put into care when the family breaks down.
6 Worry, fear and the great unhappiness these serious problems cause.

Many unplanned babies are loved and wanted when they are born. But there is the risk that they will put a heavy financial and emotional strain on the parents. Sometimes the rest of the family suffers – grandparents might be sent to an Old People's Home, or older children neglected.

Women at risk

From puberty to the menopause, every woman who has sexual intercourse without family planning is at risk of an unwanted pregnancy. Men who protest their love but are careless over family planning need to think more carefully of what their love actually means. Sadly, the people most at risk are young girls, and mothers who already have large families. It is in these two groups of mothers that there is the greatest chance of things going wrong. 'Every baby a wanted baby' is stamped on the hearts and minds of all loving couples.

Couples without children

Parenthood does not suit everyone. Why should it? Until recently, couples without children were thought odd or selfish. Now it is understood that it is much more sensible not to have a family if you do not want children.

Questions

1 **Give two other names for family planning.**
2 **What does the fall in the birthrate seem to show?**
3 **Give three advantages of family planning from the baby's point of view.**
4 **Copy out the list under the heading 'Lack of planning can lead to'.**
5 **Which two groups of women are most at risk of unwanted pregnancies?**

Methods of family planning

1 Oral contraceptives (the pill and mini-pill)

These are tablets containing either one or both of the female sex hormones. They prevent pregnancy by making changes in the ovaries and womb. They can only be given by the family doctor or at the family planning clinic. The tablets are taken for three weeks; during the fourth week the woman has her period. There is a very slight risk of heart and blood trouble, so the woman must go for regular check-ups. Oral contraceptives are not advised for women over thirty-five, women who smoke, or women who are overweight. They are a very safe contraceptive.

2 Intra-uterine devices (the IUD, loop, coil, copper-7)

These are small bits of plastic sometimes containing copper fitted inside the womb by the family doctor or at the family planning clinic. A small thread is left hanging at the top of the vagina so the woman can check the IUD is still in place. In a few women it causes pain and bleeding and has to be removed. The doctor will advise when it needs changing. It has to be removed when a couple decide they wish to start a family. It is a very safe form of contraception.

3 Rhythm or natural method

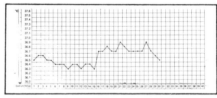

This is based on the woman's monthly cycle, or 'rhythm'. Love-making only happens when there is no egg in the oviduct. The woman must go to the clinic and be taught how to work out her own monthly calendar. This method works best in women with very regular periods. Its safety depends upon careful timing. It is 'natural' as nothing else has to be used.

4 The condom (sheath)

This is a thin sheath of rubber rolled over the erect penis. The semen is trapped in the small bulge at the tip of the condom. The man must remove his covered penis carefully before his erection dies down or some liquid may escape inside the woman's vagina. It is one of the most popular methods of contraception as condoms can be bought easily. Some local councils allow free condoms to poor families. It is quite reliable (a) if the man is very careful, and (b) if the woman also uses a spermicide.

5 The diaphragm (cap)

This is a rubber cap which fits over the neck of the womb. The woman must go to her family doctor or family planning clinic because she must be fitted with the right-sized cap and shown how to use it. It must not be removed till eight hours after love-making; it should also be used with a spermicide. This makes sure no live sperms can get around the edges of the cap, and the rest of the sperms are killed. It is quite reliable as a method of contraception.

6 Spermicides (barrier creams, foams, tablets)

A spermicide is a killer of sperms. The woman puts the cream or tablet high up in the vagina. For extra precaution, spermicides should always be used when (a) the man is wearing a sheath, or (b) the woman is wearing a cap. Spermicides used on their own as a contraceptive are not very safe.

7 Withdrawal

The man withdraws his penis just before he ejaculates. Many young couples use this method when they first start making love. This is not safe as a tiny amount of semen leaves the penis when it first enters the vagina. There are millions of sperms in this tiny drop. Also, it is often quite difficult for a young man to control his ejaculation. Love-making can be spoiled by both partners' fear of an unwanted pregnancy.

8 Sterilization

The sperm-carrying tubes in the man or the oviducts in the woman are cut and tied back. This is a very safe form of contraception but is only for older couples who already have a family.

9 Two recent methods

A sponge soaked in spermicide can now be used instead of the diaphragm. Women may prefer this, as the sponge does not have to be specially fitted. Special higher doses of the contraceptive pills can be given soon after love-making – 'morning after' pills. They have unpleasant side effects and are only used in an emergency.

Questions

1 **Name three groups of women for whom oral contraception is not advised.**
2 **Write down two disadvantages of the IUD.**
3 **Name two precautions the couple must take when using the condom.**
4 **What is a spermicide?**
5 **List the methods which involve the woman in going to her family doctor or the family planning clinic.**

Sexually transmitted diseases (STDs)

STDs (venereal diseases) are the harsher side of love. In the under-nineteen-year olds, they have risen steadily in recent years.

1 **Gonorrhoea**
Men: Burning pain when passing water; smelly discharge from penis.
Women: Heavy discharge, some pain; but seventy per cent have no symptoms.
If the disease is not treated, bacteria breed in the sperm tubes and oviducts. These get blocked and the person becomes sterile. Gonorrhoea is rising steadily amongst young people.

2 **Non-specific urethritis (NSU)**
Men only: The same symptoms as gonorrhoea, but it is not understood what causes it. If untreated, NSU can lead to infections of the eyes, skin, and mouth, and to painful diseases of the joints. NSU is also on the increase among young people.

3 **Pelvic inflammatory disease (PID)**
Women only: Acute or burning pain caused by infection of the oviducts. It is caused by bacteria which attack the oviducts, making them swollen and very sore. If untreated, PID blocks the oviducts and the woman becomes sterile. PID is also on the increase among young women.

4 **Herpes**
These look rather like 'cold sores' on or inside the sex organs. Herpes are caused by virus germs and can be very difficult to cure. The sores may vanish but then re-appear at regular intervals. It is thought they cause other damage, especially in women. Herpes is increasing at an alarming rate among young people.

5 **Syphilis**
Men: Painless sore on sex organs which vanishes after a few weeks.
Women: Painless sore on or inside the sex organs which also vanishes.
If untreated, the bacteria enter the blood stream and cause hidden damage. Later in life this leads to insanity, blindness, paralysis, and eventually death. Syphilis is now on the decrease.

6 **Trichomonas vaginalis**
Women only: yellow smelly discharge; pain, itchiness, sore sex organs. If untreated, the condition becomes chronic (permanent low infection).

7 **Warts**
These look like tiny cauliflowers on the sex organs, and are caused by virus germs. Any infection of the sex organs must be treated immediately to stop other germs getting in (secondary infection).

8 **Scabies**
Tiny parasites which burrow under the skin and lay eggs. They breed quickly in warm damp areas of the body. There is a risk of secondary infection.

9 **Candidiosis (thrush)**
Men: Penis red and sore at tip. Men rarely have it.
Women: Thick discharge, sore and itchy vagina.
Thrush is not always caught sexually. It is a fungus infection which can be caused by other things, e.g. certain medicines. If untreated, the condition becomes chronic.

10 **AIDS**
AIDS is short for Acquired Immune Deficiency Syndrome. The AIDS virus attacks and destroys the body's defence system which protects it from disease. The virus is transmitted when the blood or semen of an infected person comes into contact with the body fluids of another. This can happen during any form of sexual intercourse, when unscreened blood is transfused, or when drug abusers share needles.

Facts about STDs
1 STDs are passed directly from one person to another. They are not caught from toilet seats or towels – the germs die when not on the human body.
2 Gonorrhoea, herpes and syphilis can all damage the baby, either before or during birth.
3 STDs are treated at special clinics attached to most hospitals. Many people prefer not to go to their family doctor, though treatment is private in both places.
4 People who start their sex life early and who have many changes of partners are at much greater risk of catching an STD.
5 Most STDs can be cured if they are treated as soon as the symptoms are noticed. The longer the person waits, the more difficult the treatment.
6 A person can be a 'carrier' without having any symptoms. Love-making must stop immediately if the partner notices something wrong. Both people should go to the special clinic for a check-up.
7 Pain on passing water, or an unpleasant discharge, do not necessarily mean the person has an STD. But both these symptoms show something is going wrong which needs to be put right.
8 For any worry, a visit to the special clinic is helpful. This is especially so for women if they fear there is a chance of disease inside the vagina, which they cannot see. If there is no cause for alarm, the visit is not wasted. Peace of mind about personal health is very important indeed.
9 Using a condom during sexual intercourse greatly reduces the risk of catching an STD.

Questions

1 **What are the symptoms of gonorrhoea?**
2 **What happens if (a) NSU and (b) PID are not treated?**
3 **Where do people go for treatment of an STD?**

Further work on Chapter 2

1   Find out the age of majority in Canada, China, Russia, India. Name at least three things a person who is under-age is not entitled to do.

2   What is the difference between the length of a man's fertile life and a woman's fertile life?

3   Draw up a list of rules of hygiene for a teenager.

4   Do you agree that for most people 'Hell's Despair' is being unloved? Give reasons for your answer.

5   What do you consider are the most important qualities in (a) a future husband, and (b) a future wife? Why?

6   Can you think of reasons why marriage has a better chance of lasting if the couple are not too young?

7   If possible, visit a register office. Copy out the exact vows the couple make to each other.

8   Copy out the marriage vows taken in a religious ceremony in one of the following: synagogue, church, mosque, chapel, temple.

9   Can you think of any reasons why people might marry when they are not in love?

10 Give reasons why you consider some young girls are at risk of unwanted pregnancies.

11 Visit your local family planning clinic, or write with a stamped addressed envelope for their leaflets. Study the contents and learn at least three methods of contraception.

12 A couple are far too shy to go to a family planning clinic. What reliable method of contraception could they both use by shopping at the chemist's?

13 Re-read the pages on sexually-transmitted diseases. Why is faithfulness so important between couples, from a health point of view?

14 (a)   What is contraception? Why is it used?
    (b)   Explain fully the following methods:
          (i)   intra-uterine device
          (ii)   oral contraceptive pill
          (iii)   condom or sheath
          (iv)   rhythm method   (WMEB)

15 (a)   What is the average age for the onset of puberty in the female?
    (b)   Until what age does the average woman remain fertile?
    (c)   How long is the average menstrual cycle?
    (d)   Describe the normal menstrual cycle from commencement of menstrual flow to the breakdown of the uterine lining ready for the next cycle to begin.   (WMEB)

16 Which considerations should a young couple discuss and settle before marriage?
    What problems can result from lack of such discussion?   (SREB)

Chapter 3

The beginning of human life

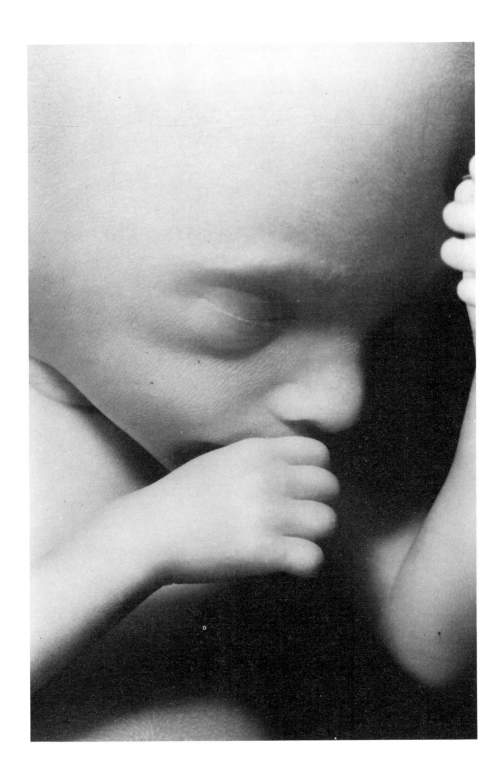

How human life begins

The male reproductive (sex) cells

Sperms are incredibly tiny. It is estimated there may be up to 200,000,000 in each emission of semen. They look rather like tadpoles, with their round bodies and wriggling tails. They move forward by lashing their tails to and fro.

The female reproductive (sex) cells

Eggs are much larger than sperms – about the size of a full stop. A single ovum looks huge in comparison with the sperms. They have outer walls for protection which one sperm must penetrate (break through). They cannot move, but are pushed along by the muscles of the oviduct.

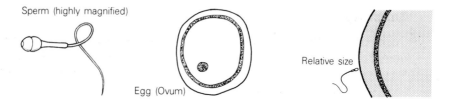

Sperm (highly magnified)

Egg (Ovum)

Relative size

Fertilization

1 Each time a man comes (ejaculates), millions of sperms are shot from the tip of his penis up inside the woman's vagina.
2 The sperms need all the nourishing fluid in semen for they have a very long way to travel.
3 They must swim up through the tiny opening in the cervix, up through the womb, and on into the oviduct to meet the egg.

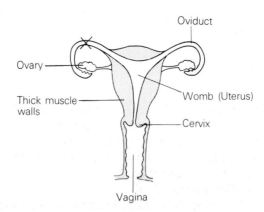

Oviduct

Ovary

Thick muscle walls

Womb (Uterus)

Cervix

Vagina

4 X marks the place where the sperms and egg meet.
5 Only one sperm can penetrate the walls and, as soon as this happens, the walls form a tough outer shell.
6 The sperm moves to the centre of the egg and the two sex cells fuse together: they become one.
7 This is fertilization; it is also called conception.

Implantation

The single fertilized cell begins to grow by dividing into 2, then 4, 8, 16, 32 and so on. It does this while travelling down the oviduct to the womb. Tiny fronds from the rich lining of the womb are attached to tiny fronds from the growing cell. It is rather like a bulb being planted in moist rich earth; hence the name, implantation. Once this has safely happened, conception is complete. A baby is on the way.

Ectopic pregnancy

In rare cases, the fertilized cell stays in the oviduct instead of being moved down to the womb. Usually it dies and the few cells are swept away. If it does begin to grow, the mother is taken to hospital and the tiny clump of cells removed.

Miscarriage

Occasionally, after implantation the new life breaks away from the lining of the womb, and is passed down the vagina like a very heavy period. This is a miscarriage. About half of all miscarriages happen because there is something wrong with the fertilized egg.

Abortion

Abortion is the deliberate removing of a new life from the mother's womb. Abortions are offered to mothers with damaged babies (p. 178). They may also be wanted by women who have unplanned pregnancies: women who are not ready to start a family, or women who do not want any more children. Abortion is a highly emotional subject. It is concerned with rights: the right of the unborn to life as opposed to the right of the woman to freedom of choice. This may sound simple, but it is a very deep and complicated matter. Abortion is distressing, whichever side people are on. Sadly, some women have to face this problem alone.

Questions

1 **How many sperms are released at one ejaculation?**
2 **Describe the journey taken by the sperm after leaving the penis.**
3 **Where does fertilization actually take place?**
4 **In your own words, describe what happens at fertilization.**
5 **What is meant by 'implantation'?**
6 **What is meant by 'conception'?**
7 **Explain the difference between an abortion and a miscarriage.**
8 **Can you think of reasons why some women have to face the problem of abortion on their own?**

The unborn baby

The embryo

For the first two months, the new life is called an embryo. Different cells are made: blood cells, bone cells, muscle cells, and so on. By eight weeks, the tiny heart has been beating for almost a month. Soft bone, the lungs, liver, stomach, and brain are being formed. There are palm and footprints; even the nails are beginning to grow. At eight weeks, the embryo is between 3 and 4 cm long and weighs about one gram.

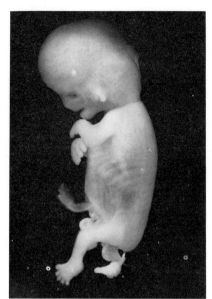

Seven-week-old embryo.

The foetus

During the next seven months, the unborn baby is called a foetus. It will grow from 3 cm to about 50 cm in length, by birth. Its weight will increase from one gram to about three kilograms, at birth. All the organs will develop, growing bigger and stronger.

From the fifth month, the heart can be heard beating through a stethoscope or, at home, through a rolled tube of cardboard. The baby moves freely: both parents can see the mother's skin bulge where an arm or leg is kicking out. Some babies suck their thumbs, some yawn, stretch out, get hiccups, swallow a little of the 'waters'.

The amniotic sac

This is the bag of waters which breaks when labour begins. At first, the baby floats around; later there is not much room to move. The water cushions the baby from harm by acting as a buffer.

The placenta

This grows out from the lining of the womb during implantation. It is soft and spongy, and crammed full of tiny blood vessels. Some of the blood vessels are the baby's; some are the mother's.

As the foetus grows larger, so does the placenta. At birth it weighs about 450 grams and is about 20 cm across. It looks like a very dark red sponge, about the size of a dinner plate. The placenta's work is to pass oxygen, food and hormones from the mother's blood to the baby's. It also picks up waste things such as carbon dioxide and urine from the baby's blood and takes them into the mother.

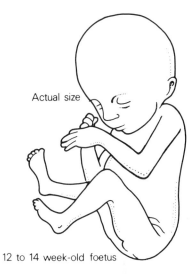

Actual size

12 to 14 week-old foetus

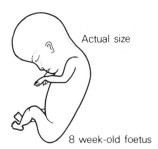

Actual size

8 week-old foetus

The umbilical cord

This develops with the placenta, in the first months of embryo life. It grows out from the placenta and along to the baby's stomach wall. At birth, it is about 50 cm long, with a whitish-blue covering. Inside are three blood vessels which pump blood between mother and baby.

How the unborn baby gets nourishment

The unborn baby cannot breathe air into its lungs, nor put food into its mouth. In the placenta, these things are passed through fine layers of skin called membranes from the mother's blood to the baby's.

 The baby's blood vessels collect up into the vein in the umbilical cord. The rich blood full of oxygen and food is taken to the foetal heart and pumped around the baby's body. The good things are used up and waste things are dumped into the cord. They go back into the placenta, where the waste is removed and more oxygen and food are picked up. The mother's and baby's blood do not mix. They are separate systems.

Questions

1 **What is meant by an embryo? Describe what happens during this stage.**
2 **What is a foetus? When can the foetal heart first be heard beating?**
3 **What is the amniotic sac? What is its function?**
4 **In your own words, describe what the placenta looks like.**
5 **Describe the umbilical cord.**
6 **Trace the passage of food from the placenta to the baby's body.**
7 **'The mother's and baby's blood do not mix.' Explain what this means as simply as you can.**
8 **What is the birthweight and the length at birth of the average baby?**

Things which harm the unborn baby

The placenta is a good filter, keeping harmful things back. But certain damaging substances can, and do, pass through to the baby. In Australia, Western Europe, the UK, and the USA, young men and women are seriously disabled today, because their mothers were given a drug called thalidomide to stop early morning sickness. Sadly, the drug stopped the growth of limbs as well.

The baby is most at risk of damage to his development during the embryo stage. But the average time of going to the doctor to have a pregnancy confirmed is after two missed periods. When babies are planned, women can keep away from harmful things during this time.

Drugs

The drug counter at the chemist's should be avoided. If the mother feels unwell, she should ask her doctor's advice. Vitamins and iron tablets should be taken, if advised. Women on long-term drugs should go to their doctor as soon as they first suspect they might be pregnant.

Alcohol

A lot of alcohol in pregnancy is now known to damage the unborn baby. More than two glasses of wine a day, or the equal amount of alcohol in other drinks, is not considered safe. Also accidents, such as tripping over, can happen when people have drunk too much. To avoid these risks, expectant mothers who drink heavily must do their best to cut down.

Smoking

1 A woman who smokes is more likely to have a miscarriage than a non-smoker.
2 She is more likely to have a premature baby.
3 She is more likely to lose her baby in childbirth.
4 On average, her baby will be about 150 to 250 grams (5 to 9 oz) lighter.
5 By the age of seven, her child may be smaller and doing less well at school.
6 If she gives up smoking when she knows she is pregnant, she need not worry that her earlier smoking will harm her baby.
7 Fathers-to-be can help by giving up smoking too. This is the sort of truly loving support a smoking mother really needs.
8 Luckily, many women 'go off' cigarettes during early pregnancy.
9 But in case this does not happen, it is best for teenage girls not to start smoking so that they do not become addicted.

X-rays

X-rays can damage the foetus, but sometimes they are necessary. Special precautions will be taken if the mother explains she is pregnant.

Rubella (German measles)

Girls of 11 to 13 are now vaccinated against this damaging disease. Women who plan their babies can make sure that (a) they had the disease when they were little, or (b) they are vaccinated three months before they stop using contraception.

Questions

1 **At what stage is the unborn baby most at risk of damage to his development?**
2 **When does the average woman have her pregnancy confirmed by a doctor?**
3 **In what ways does planning a family help avoid risk to the baby?**
4 **What advice would you give to a friend expecting a baby who wanted to share your cough mixture with you?**
5 **Pregnant mothers who drink heavily are rare. But if a friend was upset and wanted lots of gin to calm her, what would you do?**
6 **Do you agree, or disagree, that a father-to-be should give up smoking?**
7 **What advice would you give a teenage girl who is already smoking?**
8 **The person who takes X-rays is called a radiographer. What should a woman who has missed one period always tell the radiographer?**

Health in pregnancy (1)

A woman's health when she is pregnant affects the health of the baby growing inside her. But a woman's health during her own childhood and before she gets pregnant affects the baby too. Most women of child-bearing age are much healthier than their mothers and grandmothers were. This is partly due to much better nutrition, and partly because a great deal more care is now taken of the pregnant mother and her baby.

Signs of pregnancy

1 Menstruation stops; there are no more periods till after the birth.
2 Tingling and swelling of the breasts.
3 More discharge may come from the vagina.
4 Passing water more often; slight constipation.
5 Feeling and/or being sick; a strange 'metal' taste in the mouth.
6 Feeling tired; needing more rest and sleep.

Not all women have all these signs. They are caused by changes in the mother's body and changes in the hormones. They are perfectly natural.

Checks on weight

The average woman puts on about 12.5 kg (around 28 lb) in pregnancy. This is due to the growing foetus, placenta, and womb, and to the amniotic fluid and extra fluid in the mother's body. Also, her breasts grow larger, and a layer of fat builds over the body to be used up later in making milk for the baby.

How much weight a woman gains is carefully checked at the antenatal clinic:

Too much weight may mean she is over-eating, or not getting enough exercise.
Too little weight can mean a poor diet, or that the baby is not growing well. In some sad cases, it means the mother is deliberately not eating enough because (a) she does not want to look fat, or (b) she worries that a large baby will be painful at labour. On both these points, her thinking is muddled. Nature stacks the cards in favour of the unborn, which seems fair because it cannot help itself. Whatever the mother eats, all the best of the nutrients will go to the baby, and though he may suffer, the mother will come off much worse. With poor nutrition she may lose her teeth, her hair and her whole general health.

The importance of diet and checks on weight

1 Checking the steady weight increase of an expectant mother gives the clinic a great deal of other useful information too.
2 It is very important that the mother eats well and is not afraid of gaining weight during her pregnancy.
3 The extra weight will be lost during breast-feeding, and with the extra hard work of looking after a baby and running around after a toddler.
4 She also needs it to give her strength during labour, and to stop the exhaustion once she becomes a mother if she is too thin.

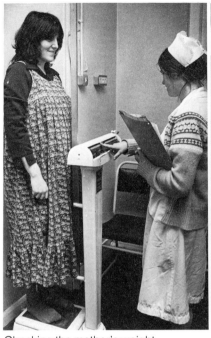
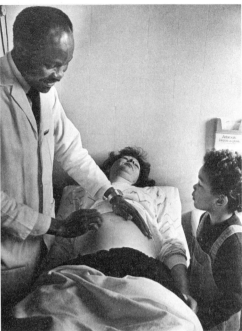

Checking the mother's weight. Checking the baby's position.

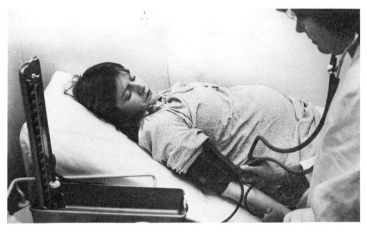

Checking the
mother's blood
pressure.

Questions

1 Give two reasons why women of child-bearing age today are healthier
than their mothers and grandmothers were.
2 Name four signs of pregnancy.
3 How much weight does the average woman put on during pregnancy?
4 Name four causes for this gain in weight.
5 Why do a few women deliberately not eat enough during pregnancy?
6 What advice would you give an expectant mother who was not eating
well?
7 Why does the clinic keep a proper check on the woman's weight? Give
three reasons why the extra weight is important for the woman when she
becomes a mother.

Health in pregnancy (2)

What to eat

1 The quality of the diet is far more important than the quantity (amount).
2 As in all nutrition a mixed diet is best.
3 This should include foods rich in protein; plenty of fresh fruit and vegetables; potatoes, unrefined rice, cereals; and some fats.
4 A mixed diet will contain enough minerals and most of the vitamins.
5 Anaemia (lack of iron in the blood) is fairly common in expectant mothers. Not enough blood cells are made to carry oxygen around the body. The symptoms of anaemia are lack of energy, tiredness, giddiness, pale skin and headaches. Iron tablets and certain vitamins will be offered by the clinic if this happens.
6 For Asian families, there is a chance of vitamin D deficiency, made worse by lack of sun in cold climates like Britain. The diet needs to be made up with extra vitamin D tablets. Cheese and milk supply the calcium needed with vitamin D to prevent rickets (p. 77) and to make strong healthy teeth and bones.

More details about diet are given on pp. 80–83.

Dental care

In most industrialized countries, mothers may have free dental treatment during pregnancy and for one or two years after. Expectant mothers should go for a dental check-up as soon as the pregnancy is confirmed.

The baby's bones are formed and his first set of teeth are already in his gums by the time he is born. If the mother lacks calcium and vitamin D, there is a risk she will lose her own teeth unless she goes for treatment. Because of the change in hormone levels, a few expectant mothers develop gum disease (gingivitis), which shows as streaks of blood on the toothbrush. Oral (mouth) hygiene is always important, but it is especially so during pregnancy. The infection needs to be cleared up and advice given on future hygiene.

Work, rest, exercise

An expectant woman can keep working for as long as she wishes. She is likely to be the best judge of how well she feels. Some women like to cut down and do only part-time work because they need more rest. Rest is important in pregnancy because of all the extra work the mother's body is doing. Lying down for an hour after lunch or after work is usually enough. Sleep is also important; some women find they need a lot more sleep.

Having plenty of exercise and fresh air keeps the woman healthy and fit, though rough games such as hockey are not wise. Sexual intercourse will not harm the foetus, but towards the last months the husband may need to be extra gentle and thoughtful.

Other points to consider

1 Health in pregnancy depends on other factors too.
2 The emotional, social, and economic life of the mother also matter.
3 A young single girl, with no money and no home, living on hand-outs from friends and moving from 'squat' to 'squat', is less likely to have a healthy baby and to be healthy herself.
4 A woman whose husband drinks and is violent, and who cares for her three other children by scrubbing office floors, is less likely to have a healthy baby and to be healthy herself.
5 Support from the community (p. 55) is essential if mother and baby are to do well.

Pregnancy and good health

1 Pregnancy is a time of being well, not ill.
2 The expectant mother is <u>not</u> a patient, though she might feel like one.
3 This is because clinics are usually held in hospitals and/or she may not understand the reasons for the checks and tests being done.
4 However, when the first signs of pregnancy have settled down, many mothers say they have never felt so fit before in their lives.

Questions

1 **What foods must be present in a pregnant woman's diet?**
2 **What advice on diet would you give to an Asian mother living in a cold country?**
3 **What causes anaemia, and what are the symptoms?**
4 **Give two reasons why dental treatment for expectant mothers is free in most industrialized countries.**
5 **Why is oral hygiene even more important in pregnancy?**
6 **Do you think an expectant mother should go on working? Give reasons for your answer.**
7 **'Pregnancy is a time of being well, not ill.' Do you agree, or disagree? Give reasons for your answer.**

Antenatal care

When a woman suspects she is pregnant, she goes to her family doctor. She has an internal examination; the doctor checks the cervix for other signs of pregnancy. She is given an appointment to attend the antenatal clinic. An early visit to the doctor makes it easier for the woman to remember when she had her last period, and for the doctor to estimate the date of delivery. A woman planning a family should keep a note of the date of her last menstrual period. The date of birth is 280 days or 40 weeks from the first day of the last period.

Medical history

At the clinic, the history of the woman's health, and any illness in her own or her husband's family are carefully recorded. This helps the staff to work out whether the illness might be inherited (passed down to the baby), or not. If there is a serious risk, the mother may be offered an abortion. Many parents-to-be are relieved to learn a family illness is not an inherited one.

Where there is an inheritable illness, it is better if the couple get advice from their doctor before starting their family. Genetic Counselling Clinics work out the risks of the baby inheriting the illness, and help couples to make decisions about starting a family.

Tests and checks

1   Blood is tested:
   (a)   to make sure the mother is not anaemic.
   (b)   to find out her blood group in case she needs to be given blood later on.
   (c)   to check she has had rubella (German measles, p. 93).
   (d)   to check for syphilis, which will damage the foetus (p. 38).
   (e)   to check for spina bifida – a disease affecting the baby's spine.
   (f)   to check for the Rhesus factor (see below).
2   Gonorrhoea can be tested for by checking the discharge from the vagina. Mothers who are worried should ask for this test.
3   Urine is tested for certain diseases such as diabetes.
4   Hormones in the mother's blood and urine will give clues to the unborn baby's progress.
5   Height and weight are recorded. Weight is checked regularly.
6   Tests to check the baby's progress are also done, such as monitoring the foetal heart: listening to and counting the baby's heart-beats.

Other tests

1   *Ultrasound*   High frequency sound waves give a picture of the foetus. They may be used to see if the baby is growing well and to get a better idea of the date for delivery. They are also called 'foetal scans'.
2   *Amniocentesis*   A sample of the amniotic fluid is drawn up by needle through the uterine wall. This is done when there is reason to fear the baby is not developing properly: when there may be some handicap.

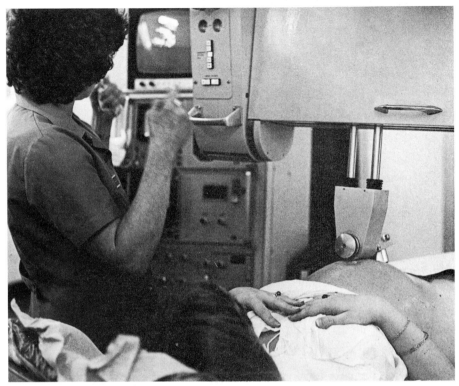

This woman is having a foetal scan.

The Rhesus factor

There is a factor in blood which is either Rhesus positive (Rh+) or Rhesus negative (Rh−). Only 15% of women are Rh−. Their blood may be incompatible with the baby's. First babies are not affected as mother's and baby's blood do not mix (p. 45). But during childbirth, there is a chance that the two bloods will mix when the placenta is shed. The mother's blood then builds up resistance (antibodies) which might damage any babies she has later on. After the first baby is born she is given injections of a special antibody to stop this happening.

In the rare cases where the Rh− factor is not detected, the baby is given a complete exchange of blood by transfusion.

Questions

1 **The first day of a woman's last menstrual period was 1 January. Work out the expected date for her delivery.**
2 **What help can a couple ask for if they know there is an inherited illness in either of their families?**
3 **Give three reasons why the mother's blood is tested.**
4 **Give two reasons why the mother's urine is tested.**
5 **What does 'monitoring the foetal heart' mean?**
6 **What is ultrasound? Why is it sometimes used?**

The importance of early antenatal care

When a woman's pregnancy is confirmed:

1. She may visit the dentist for free dental treatment.
2. She can apply for free milk, free vitamins and free prescriptions.
3. She knows her bed is safely booked – all first babies are usually born in hospital, though later babies may be born at home.
4. She goes to antenatal classes for exercises and to learn special breathing techniques for easier childbirth; and also to learn about child care.
5. She gets to know the staff and some of the other women attending the clinic. Loving menfolk do their best to attend as well.
6. All this helps relieve any fears she may have about herself or the baby.

With good antenatal care, deaths in mothers are now very rare. Perinatal mortality (p. 12) has also dropped enormously. But sadly, the number of babies who die at birth, or before their first birthday, is still much too high. Some babies are born with mental or physical disabilities which could have been avoided.

A recent study shows that the perinatal death rate is five times higher in babies of mothers who are late in 'booking'. 'Booking' means having the pregnancy confirmed by the doctor and making arrangements for where the baby is to be born.

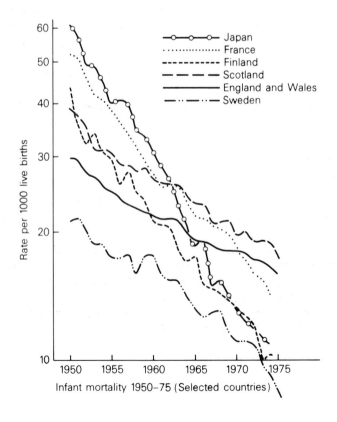

Infant mortality 1950–75 (Selected countries)

Reasons for late booking

1 Not knowing about antenatal care.
2 Not understanding how important it is.
3 Not being able to afford travelling time or expense (working mothers, poor mothers).
4 Being a young single girl and terrified of parents finding out.
5 Being too confused and unhappy over an unwanted pregnancy to care what happens.
6 Having children already, and thinking one pregnancy is much like another.

Another aspect of antenatal care

As well as looking after the physical health of mother and unborn baby, antenatal care is concerned with emotional health too. At the clinic, the mother-to-be meets other women in her own situation; this often helps her accept the idea of becoming a mother. The nursing staff's concern over her and the baby often helps to switch on the mother's own concern. If the mother is in trouble, some of her problems can be sorted out by different people working in health and welfare.

People the mother may meet

1 The *family doctor* (GP is short for general practitioner) is usually the first person the mother-to-be sees. Her pregnancy is confirmed and she is given a certificate of expected confinement.
2 The *midwife* may be a fully trained nurse with extra qualifications in childbirth. She sees the mother before, during, and for a few days after the birth.
3 The *health visitor* is a fully trained nurse with extra qualifications in child care and general family health. She visits the family regularly after the birth, and when her help is needed.
4 The *social worker* is trained in the welfare of the family and the community. She gives advice and practical help to families in difficulty.
5 The *paediatrician* is a doctor who specializes in children. She will be called if there is something wrong with the new baby.

Questions

1 **Why are deaths of mothers in childbirth now very rare?**
2 **Study the chart. List the countries in order of those with the best record for preventing infant mortality.**
3 **Give two reasons for the importance of *early* antenatal care.**
4 **Write down three reasons why women may be late for booking.**
5 **In your own words, explain how antenatal care is concerned with the pregnant mother's emotional health.**
6 **Copy out the list of people the mother may meet. Learn the function of each person in helping the new family.**

Labour

Position of the foetus

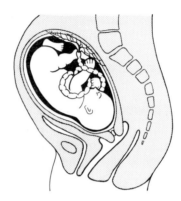

At some time during the last four weeks before birth, the foetus turns so that its head is against the neck of the womb. This is the best position for the baby to be born: head first. Only three per cent of babies do not get into this position. A breech birth is when the baby lies feet or bottom first.

The signs of labour

1 *Contractions begin*   The muscles of the womb shorten and thicken; early contractions come at intervals of ten to fifteen minutes.
2 *A show of blood*   The bag of waters separates from the wall of the womb causing a small 'show' of blood to pass down the vagina.
3 *Waters breaking*   The bag of waters breaks, and the amniotic fluid flows or trickles down the vagina.

The first stage of labour

This is the longest part, especially for a first baby. Any time from one to twenty-four hours is normal after the contractions begin. At antenatal classes, mothers are taught to time their early contractions which feel like low backache. They are also told to have a suitcase ready packed with night clothes, slippers, a house coat and toilet things. As the first stage of labour is so long and early pains are mild, there is usually enough time to contact the father, and for both parents to arrive at the hospital calmly. If the mother is alone and without any contacts, she must telephone for an ambulance at the first signs of labour.

As the first stage of labour progresses, the contractions come much more quickly and can be quite painful. Many mothers nowadays prefer not to use painkillers. They want to be alert; they do not want their baby drugged either. They rely on the exercises and special breathing techniques taught at the antenatal classes to ride over the painful contractions. However, it is important for all mothers to know that painkillers will be offered. It is easier to be brave and have less fear of pain once this fact is clearly understood. The first stage of labour ends when the neck of the womb is fully dilated (completely open).

The second stage of labour

1 This is the actual birth.
2 It is fairly quick, and is usually over in under an hour.
3 It is the hard work part of labour, as the baby has to be pushed out.
4 The mother and midwife work together, the midwife checking the baby's progress and telling the mother when to push.
5 The baby's head appears first. The rest of his body follows easily.

The third stage of labour

1 The 'afterbirth' is pushed out of the womb within the next ten to twenty minutes.
2 The placenta, umbilical cord, and membranes make up the afterbirth.
3 The midwife examines the afterbirth to make sure it has all come away.
4 A new placenta, cord, and amniotic sac are grown specially for each new baby.

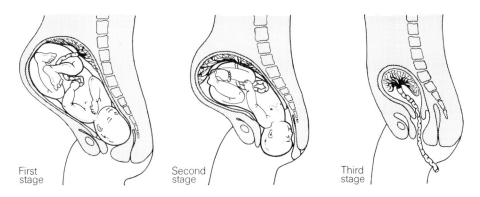

First stage

Second stage

Third stage

Induction

If the baby is overdue, or if there are other medical reasons which make it necessary, labour may be induced. This means that it is started artificially rather than naturally: either by breaking the membranes of the amniotic sac, or by giving the mother a hormone which makes the uterus contract.

Caesarian section

If for some reason the baby cannot be born in the usual way, or if labour is not progressing smoothly, a Caesarian section may be used. A cut is made across the mother's abdomen and the baby is delivered through the wall of the uterus.

Questions

1 **Copy out the signs of labour.**
2 **Which is the longest part of labour? What is the normal length of time?**
3 **Why do many mothers prefer not to use painkillers nowadays?**
4 **What do mothers rely on instead?**
5 **What has happened at the end of the first stage of labour?**
6 **Explain what happens at the second stage of labour.**
7 **What is meant by the 'afterbirth'?**

Birth

Birth as labour and love

Birth is called labour because it is hard physical work. But it is hard work too on the mind and the emotions. The mother has to be calm and relaxed; she has to put into practice all she learned at the antenatal classes.

It is lovely for the mother to have her man close by. She feels comforted because he is there; she is more able to relax. He wipes her sweating forehead and rubs her tired back. He holds her hands, squeezing tightly, wanting to share all her pains. These acts of love and tenderness bring the couple closer together. The father can understand for himself what birth actually means.

At birth

The baby is checked immediately for breathing, and the cord is clamped. He is put on his mother's stomach or at her breast. Both parents share the excitement of examining their own child together. Close contact at this early stage helps parents fall in love. 'How beautiful!' they say, gazing down at the tiny wrinkled scrap of humanity. He is their creation; between them they have made this new life.

The new-born

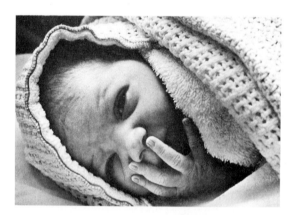

1 The average baby weighs 3–3.5 kg.
2 He may not look at all beautiful – except in parents' eyes.
3 He may have wrinkled skin with red blotches on it, 'stork bites'.
4 He may be covered in vernix, a whitish cream, which protected his skin from the waters.
5 There may be soft fine hair, lanugo, all over his body.
6 These things disappear within the first days of life.

The low birthweight baby

1 The low birthweight baby weighs less than 2.5 kg.
2 He may be too small because he is premature (born before the 36th week of pregnancy); or because he was underfed while in the womb.

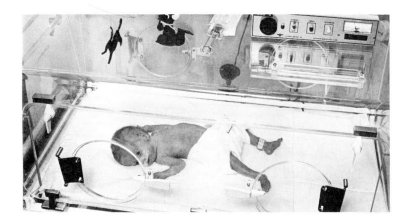

3 The too-small baby is at risk. There may be respiratory distress (breathing problems), jaundice (liver problems), hypothermia (cold problems, p. 90), and serious risk of catching an infection.
4 He will be kept in an incubator in the Premature Baby Unit and receive intensive nursing care.
5 Parents, especially mothers, need to visit the baby as often as possible.

After-care

Having a baby is one of the most fantastic experiences ever. But it is not unusual for mothers to have upset feelings later on. This is called post-natal depression, and is partly caused by the change in the work of the hormones. The other part may be caused by a difficult birth, an exhausted mother, a cold, impersonal hospital, or a father who is uncaring.

It is important that new mothers are helped with upset feelings. A safe physical delivery is not enough if the mother turns against the baby. Mothers, and fathers, need to fall in love with their babies as soon as possible. The earlier love begins, the safer the new family will be at home.

Fathers and other people in the family need to know that 'baby blues' are quite common. The mother needs help and support. When she arrives home, she must expect her whole world to be turned upside down. She cannot go on being the perfect wife and housewife while she is learning how to be a mother. If she tries, she will become exhausted. This may lead to a really bad attack of post-natal depression. Mothers need to feel freed from other demands so they can 'give' themselves to their babies. This 'giving' is called bonding (p. 141).

Questions

1 **Name two advantages of the father being present during labour.**
2 **What does the average baby weigh? What does a premature baby weigh?**
3 **In your own words, explain what is meant by 'post-natal depression'.**
4 **What special care is given to a premature baby, and why?**
5 **What advice would you give to a very tired new mother who worries about the net curtains being slightly dirty?**
6 **The National Childbirth Trust has done much to improve the experience of birth. Contact them and do a full project on the importance of their work.**

More facts on the beginning of human life

Family likeness

In the middle of human cells are 23 <u>pairs</u> of chromosomes (46 altogether). On each single chromosome are hundreds of genes. Family likeness is inherited from the genes on the chromosomes.

Equal shares

Sperms only have 23 <u>single</u> chromosomes.
Eggs only have 23 <u>single</u> chromosomes.
At fertilization, the 23 single chromosomes from sperm and egg link up to form the 23 <u>pairs</u> of chromosomes (46 altogether).
This is how a new human life inherits equal shares of family likeness from both parents.

Dominant and recessive genes

Sometimes it is easy to see what people have inherited: fine straight red hair; thick curly black hair. But many things which are inherited do not show through. This is because some genes are dominant over others: thick curly black hair is dominant over red hair. In later generations, the recessive genes for red hair may show through, if one of the children or grandchildren marries a person with red hair. The study of genetics is very complicated because what people inherit is controlled by so many genes.

Boy or girl?

The man's sperm has a Y chromosome for a boy, or an X chromosome for a girl. The woman's egg only has an X chromosome for a girl. At fertilization, a boy has XY on his chromosomes; a girl has XX on hers. It seems to be chance whether a 'girl' sperm or a 'boy' sperm gets to the egg first.
For every 100 white girls born, there are about 105 white boys.
For every 100 black girls born, there are about 102 black boys.
It is not known why there are more baby boys than girls.

Twins

Identical twins develop after one sperm has fertilized one egg. For some reason, the fertilized egg splits into two identical eggs. They grow together in the womb, sharing the same placenta. Identical twins are always the same sex.

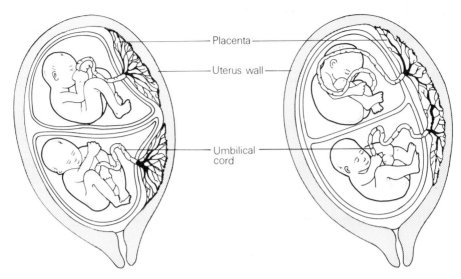

Fraternal twins.   Identical twins.

Fraternal twins develop when two sperms fertilize two different eggs. For some reason, the mother's ovaries shed two eggs in one month. They grow together in the womb, with two separate placentas. Fraternal twins can be either sex because they come from two different sperms and two different eggs.

The chance of having twins of either kind is passed on in families, once in every 87 to 100 births.

Triplets are born once in every 7,569 births and sextuplets (6 babies) once in every 5,000,000,000 births.

Infertility

Some couples are not able to produce babies. There may be something wrong with the man's sperms, the woman's egg, or the tubes along which sperms and eggs pass. There are other reasons for infertility which are very complicated.

The couple are advised first by their family doctor. Later, they may visit an infertility clinic. New techniques are constantly being discovered to enable couples to have the children they long for so much.

Questions

1 **How many chromosomes are there in one egg?**
2 **How many chromosomes are there after the sperm has fertilized the egg?**
3 **Explain in your own words how a new human life inherits equal shares of genes from both parents.**
4 **Look up the words 'dominant' and 'recessive'. Are the dominant or the recessive genes more likely to show through?**
5 **What decides the sex of the baby?**
6 **Explain as carefully as you can why identical twins will always be the same sex.**
7 **Copy the diagrams of twins and learn their differences.**
8 **What is meant by 'infertility'?**

Preparing baby things (1)

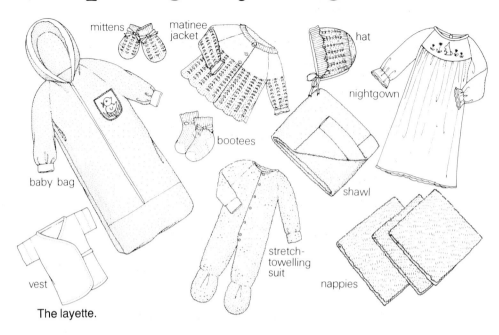

The layette.

(labels: mittens, matinee jacket, hat, nightgown, bootees, baby bag, shawl, stretch-towelling suit, vest, nappies)

Clothes

Clothes should be:
1 Made of a soft material so they do not scratch delicate skins.
2 Warm, light in weight, and roomy enough to be comfortable.
3 Washable in the washing-machine, and not need ironing.
   Suitable fabrics include Viyella, Clydella, Winceyette, stretch terry towelling, cotton, cotton jersey, and washable knitteds.

Points to remember

1 Dress the baby for the weather: loose cool clothing in summer, loose warm clothing in winter. All-in-one suits or baby-bags are useful for a winter baby as there are no gaps to let in cold air.
2 Garments should not be too tight around wrists and neck.
3 Shawls with too many lacy holes can trap a baby's fingers.
4 Loose ribbons and pretty woollen ties are not wise either.
5 A baby is likely to dribble, chew, and be sick on any garment, whatever it costs.
6 A baby outgrows the first size of clothes (the layette) very quickly.
7 Avoid shoes, no matter how cute, until the child is a toddler. Growing bones need plenty of room and exercise.

Bed clothes

1 The mattress should be firm and, if possible, washable.
2 It should fit <u>very close</u> to the tops and sides of the cot; a baby can get wedged, and stuck, if there are any gaps.
3 The mattress should be protected by a full-size waterproof sheet. The quilted kind are more comfortable and less clammy when wet.

4   Flannelette cot-sheets are warmer than cotton ones, but take longer to dry. Have plenty of sheets as they get very wet.
5   Cellular blankets are light, warm, and easy to launder.
6   Woollen blankets must be machine-washable and have smooth binding at the ends to protect the baby's skin from irritation.
7   No pillow should be used for the first year at least. Tiny babies do not have the strength to raise their heads and may suffocate.
8   A soft cloth under the baby's head will soak up any dribble.
9   A pillow is useful for an older baby only when awake. It can be propped behind the back so the baby can sit up and look around.

Bath-time equipment

1   Tiny babies can be bathed in thoroughly cleaned and well-rinsed out kitchen sinks or washing-up bowls.
2   Later, they can be held firmly in the family bath. It should be filled first so that the baby is not frightened by the noise of rushing water.
3   Small equipment should all be ready to hand. The baby will get cold if carried from room to room while forgotten items are collected.
4   Change of clothes, nappies, and towels, must be dry and warm.
5   Cotton wool, cotton swabs, baby powder, soap, shampoo, brush and comb, zinc and castor oil cream or Vaseline jelly, nail scissors, nappy pins, and liners need to be kept together in a handy container (baby basket).
6   Most babies enjoy bath-time, especially if the parent is unhurried, calm and smiling, and chatting happily about what is going on.

Questions

1   **Name three materials and say why they are suitable for baby clothes.**
2   **Give two points to remember when dressing a winter baby.**
3   **What is the danger of very lacy shawls?**
4   **Name two points to remember when choosing a mattress.**
5   **What advice would you give about choosing bed clothes?**
6   **Write down three things to remember about the use of pillows.**
7   **What preparations need to be made before a baby's bath?**

Preparing baby things (2)

The bed

A tiny baby looks quite lost in a full-size cot. The bars at the sides let in draughts; it does not seem cosy. Carry-cots, cradles, and wicker baskets are small and snug. They are easy to carry from room to room if the baby is lonely. The body part of a folding pram can be used as a cot too.

Whichever is chosen, stands must be checked for strength and stability. The cot can be removed from a wobbly stand and placed on a sturdy table.

Once the baby can sit up, a small cot is no longer safe. The full-size cot must be checked for (a) a tightly-fitting mattress, (b) lead-free paint, (c) childproof catches on the drop side, (d) correctly spaced bars: 75–100 mm apart, (e) smooth and easily-cleaned surfaces.

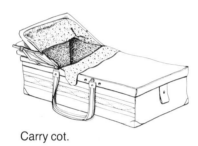
Carry cot.

Full-size cot.

The pram

1 Different prams suit different homes. A large pram is difficult to park in a narrow hallway, or to heave up lots of flights of stairs.
2 A detachable pram with a collapsing chassis is useful for travelling on buses and in cars.
3 The brakes should work on at least two wheels, and should be out of the child's reach.
4 Before buying a pram, check for good springs, height of handle, safety harness, comfortable padding, smooth and easily-cleaned surfaces.
5 Even the most stable pram will tip up once a baby can move around. He must be kept in full safety harness which goes over his shoulders and is firmly attached to the sides of the pram.

A baby should wear a safety harness in a pram.

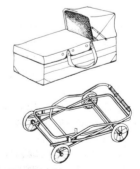
Detachable prams are easy to carry in a car.

The push-chair, the sling, and other equipment

Small babies can be carried in a sling attached to parent's shoulders. They can view the world and feel snug and close to parent. When they become too heavy, a push-chair may be necessary.

The same checks on safety and hygiene apply to all baby equipment. Other items needed for a baby include a high chair, play pen, safety gates at the top of the stairs, and fine-meshed guards protecting all fires.

The expense

1 Baby equipment is expensive if bought new, but it is often passed from family to family and amongst friends.
2 Advertisements in the local shop or enquiries at the clinic are also useful ways of getting second-hand equipment.
3 Maternity benefits are available to help with the expense.
4 All expectant mothers are entitled to claim a *maternity grant*.
5 Working mothers are entitled to a *maternity allowance* if they pay full national insurance contributions.
6 The amount of money and the time when it can be claimed vary from country to country, and from time to time.
7 Expectant mothers can ask at the antenatal clinic or the social security office for details.
8 The certificate of expected confinement (given to pregnant mothers at about twenty-eight weeks) must be produced.

Questions

1 **Give two advantages of a small cot for the new baby.**
2 **Name five things a full-size cot must be checked for.**
3 **Name five safety and hygiene checks to be made before buying a pram.**
4 **What might happen if a one-year-old is not put in a safety harness when in his pram?**
5 **In your own words, explain what is meant by 'maternity benefits'.**
6 **What is the name of the certificate which entitles an expectant mother to maternity benefits?**
7 **Write to your local health education officer or social security department to find out the details of maternity benefits for mothers having babies now.**

Further work on Chapter 3

1 Find out under what conditions a woman may have an abortion. Do you agree, or disagree, with those conditions? Discuss this in class.

2 Make up a day's diet suitable for a pregnant woman. Explain why the quality of food is more important than the quantity.

3 If a woman works till the last month of pregnancy, what advice would you give her about rest and exercise?

4 If possible, visit an antenatal clinic. Make notes of everything which you observe. Are the mothers treated like patients, or well people?

5 Using laboratory scales, find other things which weigh as little as an eight-week-old embryo. Then find things similar in weight to a new-born baby.

6 Find out about do-it-yourself pregnancy testing kits sold at chemists'.

7 Find out the amount of alcohol equivalent to two glasses of wine in lager, sherry, and gin. Visit or write to your local health education office for further information.

8 Write a short essay explaining the importance of early antenatal care.

9 Not all midwives have to be fully-trained nurses. Write to the Royal College of Midwives for details of their training and their day-to-day work.

10 Make a visit to a local mother and baby shop. Compare and contrast prams and push-chairs for safety, hygiene, and cost.

11 Make a garment for a new baby. Describe the reasons why you chose that particular fabric, and give details of how you made the garment.

12 From magazines, cut out pictures of garments suitable for a pregnant woman. Give reasons why you chose those particular clothes.

13 Do a survey of different types of cots available. Write about the one you would choose, giving details of price and safety.

14 Maternal and child health clinics help parents before and after the birth of their baby.
   (a) Name four benefits and services available for a pregnant woman.
   (b) In what three ways does a woman need help during pregnancy? In each case suggest how her husband can meet these needs.
   (c) Discuss three ways that a new-born baby may be 'at risk' and suggest how he/she may be helped.
   (d) Describe the roles of the midwife and health visitor.
   (e) What are the values to the mother and the child of regular attendance at clinics? (SWEB)

15 (a) Describe two of the signs which indicate the onset of labour.
   (b) What are contractions?
   (c) Describe clearly the second stage of labour.
   (d) What is the placenta? Why is it important that it is all delivered? (WMEB)

16 Describe and discuss the importance of antenatal care for the mother and her developing foetus. (O)

Chapter 4

Physical health: development of the body

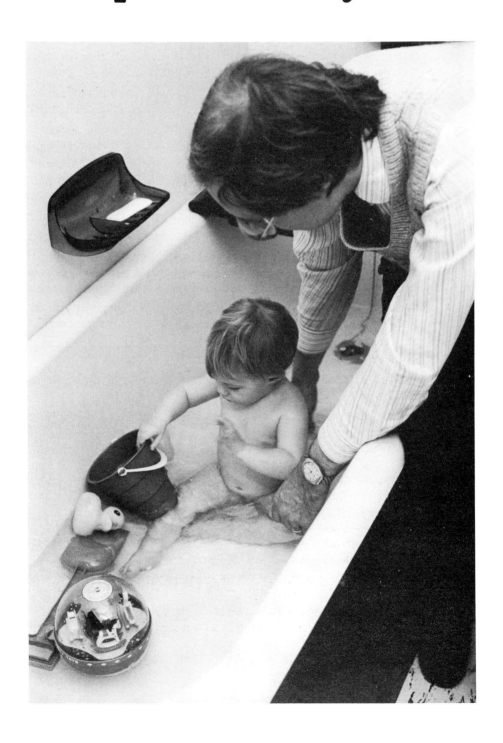

Averages, individuals, milestones

Averages

The average baby stares at faces rather than patterns at four months.
The average toddler can walk without support at eighteen months.
The average child will say about fifty words when he is two.
The average six-year-old is keen to learn reading, writing and sums.

Milestones

These averages are called 'milestones' in early human development.
Milestones are rough guidelines of what the average child can be expected to
do at certain stages of development. They are useful for doctors, parents,
health visitors, and teachers, because milestones help them know how well a
child is progressing.

Individuals

But it is important to know there is no such child as an 'average' child. Before
birth, one baby is already different from another. He has inherited genes from
both parents which make him different. His home in the womb is also different
because no one mother is exactly like another.

Siblings from a gypsy family.

Families

There is no such family as the 'average' family. By seven, the child is even more different because he lives in a different environment from any other child. This is true even of siblings (brothers and sisters) brought up in the same family. Siblings are different from one another because their place in the family is different, and because they inherit different patterns of genes from their parents.

Unique

Every single person is unique. Some babies sleep a lot; others are more wide-awake. A perfectly healthy child may not start walking until he is two. But the same child may know fifty words at eighteen months. These two examples show a natural variation in an average child's progress. It is common sense to expect some variation from child to child.

Unwise judgements

The individuality of each child must be understood, and respected. But some people make unwise judgements which upset parents and child. No one blames a child for not growing tall quickly, but he may be called 'dim' and 'stupid' because he cannot do up buttons quickly. It is important to remember a child is not necessarily 'advanced' if he learns a skill more quickly than another child. Nor is that same child necessarily 'backward' if he takes longer. Milestones are guides, not rules. Calling a child 'dim' slows down his development.

Checking for milestones

During the first years of life, milestones are checked regularly by the staff at the clinic. Parents with worries can ask advice and be reassured that nothing is wrong. Only when a child is too far behind the average stage of progress are there likely to be any further tests. Even then, the parents will often be told there is nothing wrong. When there is a hitch in development, the sooner the child is helped through the problem, the sooner he can begin to make progress again.

Questions

1 **In what ways is one new-born baby different from another?**
2 **What is meant by a 'sibling'? Why are they always different from one another?**
3 **Give two examples of natural variation in an average child's progress.**
4 **What is meant by 'milestones'?**
5 **What is the importance of taking a child to the clinic for regular checks?**
6 **'Milestones are guides, not rules.' What does this mean?**
7 **Copy out and learn the four sentences about 'Averages'.**

Breast-feeding

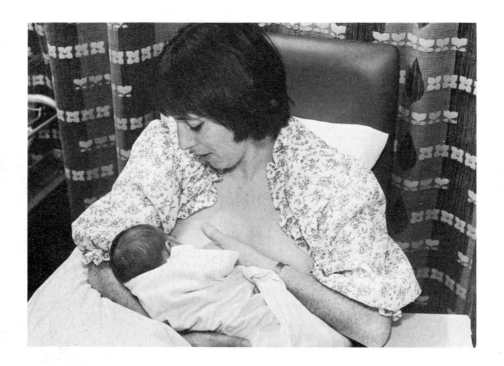

The new-born baby

1 A new baby may not seem to be very hungry.
2 But he has an urgent need to suck and to swallow (p. 108).
3 For two or three days after the baby's birth, the mother's breasts make a rich yellow liquid called colostrum, which has a high protein content.
4 Colostrum also contains antibodies – the mother's resistance to disease – which help protect the baby from certain infections.
5 A new baby put to the breast satisfies his need for sucking and swallowing.
6 The sucking action on the mother's breasts helps her womb to get back to shape; it also helps her produce milk.
7 By about the third day, the mother's milk begins to flow.
8 It looks thin and blue-ish, compared to the creamy colostrum.
9 It contains all the right nutrients for the baby in the right amounts.
10 It is more watery than colostrum which is good for the thirsty baby.

New mothers

1 New mothers need help with breast-feeding their babies.
2 Some may be nervous, others may worry that it hurts.
3 There are other worries too which mothers may be too shy to talk about.
4 A gentle patient midwife will help sort out new mothers' fears.
5 People imagine breast-feeding is the simplest thing ever.
6 But mother's and baby's emotions are involved – and when emotions are involved things can get a bit complicated.
7 No mother should ever feel guilty if the baby cries or turns away.

8 The baby has to learn to breathe through his nose while he sucks, to pace himself calmly, to settle comfortably while feeding.

9 Mothers need loving support from their husbands, and time and patience before they begin to feel confident.

10 A panicky rushed mother who is not given loving care from everyone near her quickly loses confidence and turns to bottle-feeding.

11 It is worth noting that premature and low birth weight babies <u>must</u> be fed on breast milk, as it is the perfect food and easy to digest.

12 Human milk can be stored in 'banks' rather as blood can be stored.

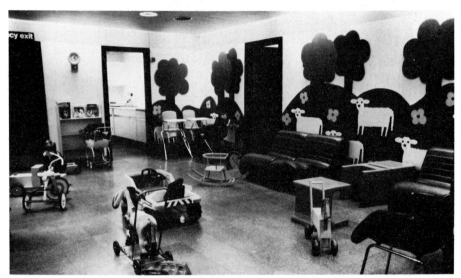

More and more public places are setting aside special areas where mothers can feed their babies in comfort and privacy. This nursery is at Heathrow Airport, London.

Breast-feeding has been unfashionable for a long time. It has only recently become popular, probably due to mothers having better information. But the mother who cannot or does not want to breast-feed should not be made to feel guilty, or less of a 'mother'. This is positively harmful; damaging her feelings about herself and her baby. The growth of love is a delicate and subtle process. It flourishes best when mothers feel confident, whichever choice they make.

Questions

1 **What has the new-born baby an urgent need to do?**
2 **What is the name of the liquid first made in the mother's breasts?**
3 **What does it look like? Name two things it contains.**
4 **Why is putting a new baby to the breast (a) good for the baby, (b) good for the mother?**
5 **What does human milk look like? Why is it more watery?**
6 **Give two reasons why new mothers may need help with breast-feeding.**
7 **Why is breast-feeding not as simple as some people think?**
8 **'All babies should be fed on breast milk.' Name two types of babies who must.**

Bottle-feeding

Father can help with bottle-feeding.

Cow's milk is not suitable for young babies; nor is goat's milk. The baby's delicate stomach cannot digest the food completely. Dried milk or 'formula' is made from cow's milk which has been specially treated so that it is as like human milk as possible. Once the parents have chosen a particular brand, it is best to stick to that one. Chopping and changing between different brands makes it difficult for the baby's system to settle down. If the parents have worries, the health visitor is ready with advice.

Making up the feed

1 All brands have detailed instructions on how to make up the feed.
2 It is essential that parents follow these instructions correctly.
3 One of the biggest mistakes parents make is to add an extra scoopful – rather like adding 'one for the pot' when making tea.
4 This makes the feed too rich and over-concentrated.
5 The baby's system cannot cope; his kidneys have to work over-time to get rid of the extra sodium.
6 He feels very thirsty as he is losing too much body fluid.
7 He cries, parents think he is hungry, he is given another over-rich feed.
8 Over-concentration or under-concentration may damage the baby's system.
9 The formula has been worked out to have exactly the right balance of food and water.
10 If the baby seems hungry after a feed, it is best to ask for advice.

The average amount

Over twenty-four hours, a baby needs 2½ oz (75 ml) of fluid per pound (500 g) of body weight. For example: a 10 lb (5 kg) baby would need 25 oz (750 ml) of milk mixture each day. The 25 oz would be divided up by the number of times he is fed during each twenty-four hours.

Sterilizing the feed

Bacteria (germs) are everywhere. They do not harm older people because the human body builds up resistance to them (except in certain diseases). A new baby has no resistance – the womb is germ-free.

Sterilizing should be automatic during the baby's first year. Bacteria on the mother's hands, the bottle, the teat, or the mixing jug breed very quickly at room temperature, and milk is the perfect medium for growing bacteria. Any lack of hygiene in making up the feed may result in gastro-enteritis, a very serious infection causing vomiting and diarrhoea (runs). In overseas countries with no proper chance to sterilize, bottle-fed babies die from this serious disease.

1 Wash hands thoroughly. Dry on clean towel.
2 The equipment: feeding bottle, funnel, teat, mixing spoon, bottle brush, and measuring jug must be sterilized.
3 Boiling for ten minutes kills off the bacteria. Teats cannot be boiled.
4 All the equipment can be sterilized in a chemical solution recommended by the midwife or health visitor.

 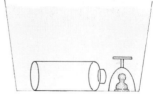

Left: The bottle and teat are not sterile. The bottle has an air-bubble in and the teat is not covered by the solution.
Right: A glass is used to hold the teat down and the bottle has no air-bubble. They are sterile.

Questions

1 **What is dried milk or 'formula' made from?**
2 **Why should parents stick to one brand, and follow the instructions exactly?**
3 **What happens if a baby is given an over-concentrated feed?**
4 **What is the average amount of milk mixture a baby needs each day?**
5 **What is the name of the illness caused by lack of sterilizing?**
6 **How long does it take to kill off bacteria by boiling?**

Breast-feeding or bottle-feeding?

	Breast-feeding	Bottle-feeding
1	Human milk suits human babies.	Not all dried milks are suitable.
2	No likelihood of allergies.	Slight risk of eczema, other allergies.
3	It is clean, and germ-free.	Equipment must be carefully sterilized.
4	Far less likely to get serious stomach upsets – gastro-enteritis.	More chance of gastro-enteritis unless great care taken with hygiene.
5	Nappy rash less likely as food is easier to digest.	Nappy rash likely when dried milk made up incorrectly.
6	Baby is less likely to get fat.	Baby may get fat if feed is made up incorrectly.
7	Mother cannot tell how much the baby gets. Baby can decide.	Mother can tell exact amount; persuades baby to finish contents of bottle.
8	Feed is there, and ready.	It must be bought, and prepared.
9	No equipment is needed.	Bottles, teats, jug, etc. needed.
10	Mother must be there for all feeds.	Fathers and others can take their turn.
11	Mother must have good diet with extra proteins and vitamins.	Mother needs good diet; extra money spent on buying dried milks.
12	There is not much privacy for feeding away from home.	Baby can be fed anywhere; must be held in person's arms.
13	Feeding on demand more likely.	Feeding on schedule more likely.

Feeding on demand

This means a baby is offered the breast when he cries for it. He does not have to wait another ten minutes, or another hour. Tiny babies do not understand about waiting; they get anxious. A baby who is offered the breast when he cries usually settles more quickly into a regular routine than a baby who has to wait.

Feeding on schedule

This means a baby is fed when the parent decides he is hungry. He may have to wait a long time: he may be given food before he is hungry. This makes it difficult for him not to grow anxious and confused. A baby who is not offered food when he cries for it takes longer to settle into a regular routine than a baby who is fed on demand.

Prop-feeding

'Prop-feeding' is when the baby is left alone with his bottle propped on a pillow so he can suck. Busy parents may want to do this, but it is terribly dangerous. The baby chokes, the milk goes down into his lungs instead of his stomach, and he drowns. Feeding is a time for mother and baby to be close together. The prop-fed baby misses his fair share of happy times with his parents.

Composition per 100 ml (3½ oz)

Nutrients	Units	Colostrum 1–5 days	Mature human milk	Mature cow's milk	SMA Gold Cap	Cow & Gate Premium
Energy	kcal	58	67	66	65	68
	kJ	240	275	270	275	284
Protein	g	2.7	1.2	3.3	1.5	1.5
Fat	g	2.9	3.8	3.7	3.6	3.82
Carbohydrate	g	5.3	7.0	4.8	7.2	7.24
Sodium	mg	48	15	58	15	18
Potassium	mg	74	55	138	56	60
Calcium	mg	31	125	44	44	40
Phosphorus	mg	14	15	96	33	27
Iron	mg	0.09	0.08	0.10	1.27	0.65
Copper	μg	50	40	30	48	Trace
Vitamin A	μg	108	58	40	79	80
Vitamin C	mg	4.4	4.3	1.6	5.8	5.5
Vitamin D (fat soluble)	μg	—	0.01	0.06	1.05	1.1

Human milk is perfectly balanced to suit human babies. Cow's and goat's milk are perfectly balanced to suit baby calves and kids.

Questions

1 Re-read the two columns comparing breast-and bottle-feeding very thoroughly. Which do you think is best for the baby; breast or bottle milk? Give as many reasons as you can for your answer.

2 Why are babies more likely to put on too much weight if they are bottle-fed?

3 Which do you think costs more, breast- or bottle-feeding?

4 What is meant by 'feeding on demand'?

5 What is meant by 'feeding on schedule'?

6 What is meant by 'prop-feeding'? In what ways is it (a) dangerous and (b) unloving?

7 Study the chart carefully. Name at least four things which do not match.

8 Copy out and learn the two sentences underneath the chart.

Mixed feeding

When to start

Milk is the only essential food for the first four to six months of life. Vitamin drops are advised after the first month but it is not clear if they are actually needed. However, most parents give them, just to be on the safe side. Babies are born with a store of iron, but this runs low after about four months. There is not enough iron in milk for the growing baby's needs. Foods rich in iron are meat, liver, and green vegetables. These are added to the diet before the baby starts to run short. Mixed feeding (milk and other foods) begins at about four months. This is called 'weaning'.

Suggestions for weaning				
	Early morning	Breakfast	Lunch	Tea
4½ months	Vitamin A, D, and C drops. Milk feed.	1–2 tsp baby rice mixed with milk from feed. Milk feed.	1–2 tsp sieved vegetables or meat or broth or proprietary baby food. Milk feed.	Milk feed, and again in late evening.
6–7 months	Vitamin A, D, and C drops. Milk feed.	Cereal with milk. Scrambled, poached or boiled egg. Milk feed.	Minced meat or fish, mashed vegetable. Junket or jelly. Diluted fruit juice or water.	Cheese or savoury sandwiches. Milk feed.

Learning about solids

1 A baby begins to bite and chew before six months. He still sucks, but biting and chewing show he is ready for new foods (soft solids).
2 He needs very small amounts; one teaspoonful at four months is enough.
3 He is likely to spit it out, wanting the comfort of breast or bottle.
4 Parents should stay calm, and try again the next day.
5 Forcing a baby may be the beginning of feeding troubles later on.
6 Between five and seven months, the milk teeth begin to appear.
7 Crunchy celery, raw carrot, sliced apple, crusts, help him chew.
8 He should never be left alone with these foods; there is a real danger that they could stick in his throat and make him choke to death (p. 98).
9 By nine months to one year, he can eat perfectly well with the family.

Care with hygiene and over-weight

1 Baby cereals are usually chosen as the first food; babies like them.
2 They are mashed up with water or milk so they are soft and mushy.

3   Care must be taken that the water or milk is thoroughly boiled first.
4   Milk is perfect for bacteria breeding; it <u>must not</u> be kept warm for hours.
5   Parents must also take care that hands, dishes, spoons are clean.
6   Sugar should not be added to cereals, otherwise the baby will develop a 'sweet tooth' and become overweight.
7   Cereals are fattening; baby rice is less fattening than other cereals.
8   Good first foods include mashed vegetables such as potatoes, yams, carrots; mashed stewed fruits and bananas mixed with milk; and chicken or beef broth.
9   Cans and jars of baby food are sterile, and just as good.
10 Extra food must be removed from cans and kept in the fridge.
11 It must be cooked for ten minutes in a clean saucepan, not just heated up for a later meal.
12 Warmed-up left-overs are perfect for germs. They <u>must</u> be properly cooked.

People from other countries

Different diets suit different people in different climates. People from hot countries moving to cold climates may lack vitamin D. Sun on bare skin helps the body make its own vitamin D. Lack of vitamin D causes rickets, a disease where the bones grow soft and bend under the child's growing weight, causing deformities. Families from hot climates moving to colder countries must make sure their diet is extra rich in vitamin D, calcium, and phosphate. Or they can ask for drops as supplements to their diet at the clinic.

Rickets has caused this child's bones to bend.

Questions

1   **What is the only essential food for new babies, and up to what age?**
2   **Name three foods which are rich in iron.**
3   **Give one reason why mixed feeding usually starts at about four months.**
4   **Why should a baby never be left alone with lumpy or chewy food?**
5   **Why should sugar not be added to cereals?**
6   **Name four good foods (not cereals or rice) which are suitable to start a baby on mixed feeding.**
7   **What special care must be taken with baby food left over in cans? Give as many reasons as you can for your answer.**
8   **What is the name of the disease caused by lack of vitamin D?**

Water

Water is essential for life. It transports food and oxygen round the body, and removes waste products. It keeps the body temperature even, and helps with chemical changes in the cells. Almost three-quarters of the body weight is made up of water.

Water control

The body carefully controls the proper balance of water. Each day, the average adult loses two to three litres: a very little from the skin in sweat; a bit more from the lungs in breathing out; and most from the kidneys in passing urine. The water which is lost must be replaced. Food supplies about half. The rest must be drunk – water, fruit juice, tea. (Drinks containing alcohol speed up the work of the kidneys and cause extra sweating.) People in hot countries, athletes and dancers, people with fevers, must all drink more water. Many teenagers are constipated – having thick hard faeces (p. 86) – because they do not take in enough water.

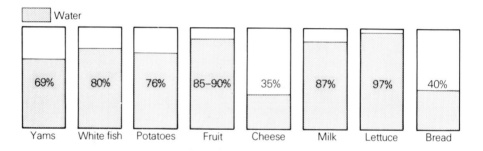

Water

Yams	White fish	Potatoes	Fruit	Cheese	Milk	Lettuce	Bread
69%	80%	76%	85–90%	35%	87%	97%	40%

Water and small children

1. A baby gets all the fluid he needs from breast milk, or correctly made-up dried milk. They both contain about 90% water.
2. At weaning (going from milk to mixed feeding), mothers must take care the baby gets enough liquids, usually in milk.
3. A toddler may grizzle because he is thirsty, not hungry.
4. From about six months of age, small children should be offered boiled water which is cooled to slake their thirst.

Dehydration

This means drying out from lack of water. Dehydration is very dangerous indeed – the body cannot work without water. Adults rarely suffer, as the mouth dries up and the person feels thirsty. Babies and small children do not understand the difference between hunger and thirst.

1. Giving a child extra food instead of water causes obesity (too much fat).
2. A baby with gastro-enteritis has diarrhoea (the runs), and may vomit.
3. A great deal of water is lost with diarrhoea, and vomiting.
4. The baby is in great danger of serious dehydration.
5. A child with a high fever is in the same great danger.

6 The body temperature goes right up; there is a lot of heavy sweating.
7 Babies also sweat a lot when they are over-heated with too many woolly clothes and blankets.

Points to consider

1 When a baby is ill, he needs extra fluids.
2 A thirsty baby will accept liquids if he is not well enough for food.
3 It is not necessary to buy expensive glucose drinks for a sick child.
4 Ordinary sugar added to boiled water is exactly the same, as the sugar changes to glucose once it is inside the baby.
5 Normally, it is not wise to add sugar to drinks because it is fattening and rots the teeth: but a sick child needs the energy from sugar.
6 Fruit juices give the vitamins the child requires – the label should be checked for vitamin content.
7 Freshly squeezed fruit with boiled water and a little sugar added make the best nourishing and refreshing drink.
8 An older child may prefer a splash of soda water added. Many children find the fizziness pleasant – hence the popularity of glucose drinks.
9 Small sips taken often will put back the water which is lost.

Questions

1 **Give three functions of water in the body.**
2 **How much water is lost from the average adult each day?**
3 **Alcoholics often become dehydrated. Why does this happen when they drink so much?**
4 **Where does a baby of two months get his supply of water from?**
5 **'Give the baby adequate fluids' is advice given by the doctor to a mother of a sick child. In your own words, describe the importance of this advice.**
6 **Name three different drinks you might make up for a child with a fever.**
7 **Find out how much water is contained in four kinds of foods which small children enjoy.**

Nutrition (1)

Nutrients are the different kinds of nourishment needed by the body. The main nutrients are proteins, carbohydrates, fats, vitamins, and minerals. However, it must be remembered that almost all foods contain more than one kind of nutrient. Human milk, for example, contains all the nutrients necessary for healthy growth in the first four months of life. This means that different foods can each do a number of different tasks in the body.

1 Proteins

A new baby grows rapidly. He doubles his birth weight by four months, and nearly triples it by one year. Body cells are constantly wearing out and new ones being made. The growth nutrients are proteins: essential for body-building, and replacing and repairing body cells.

Animal protein foods such as fish, meat, and liver are expensive. Protein from animal products such as milk, cheese, and eggs costs less. Plant protein such as pulses (beans, peas, lentils), cereals, and nuts, is much cheaper. Soya beans processed to look and taste like meat are called textured vegetable protein, or TVP. TVP is used in factory canteens, school meals, hospitals, and other large establishments. Soya milk is also made from soya beans, but it lacks the proper nutrients for a small child.

2 Carbohydrates

The baby uses energy all the time. Even when asleep, energy is needed for breathing, for the heart to pump, for waste to be taken to the kidneys, and so on. The energy-producing nutrients are carbohydrates: essential for healthy active life.

Carbohydrates are usually inexpensive as they come directly from plants. They can be simple sugars in sweets, jam, syrup, honey; they can be starches found in bread, rice, corn. The amount of energy produced by sugars or starches used to be measured in Calories; nowadays it is measured in *kilojoules*.

3 Fats

A new-born baby cannot keep himself warm (p. 90). Fats provide heat. Fats also have twice the energy value of carbohydrates. Animal fats such as butter and oily fish are more expensive than plant fats such as margarine and oil. People in very cold countries eat a lot of fat, but small children elsewhere find it difficult to digest.

Points to consider

1 Children should drink plenty of milk. Chocolate or other flavours can be added if a child suddenly goes off the taste of milk.
2 Vegans are vegetarians who do not eat even animal products such as eggs, cheese, and milk. Vegan parents must ensure a child eats a very wide variety of plant protein or the diet will lack a few of the essential nutrients.
3 Children need starches and sugars for energy, but too much can be fattening, addictive (causing craving), and bad for the teeth.
4 Milk has a slightly sweet taste from its sugar (lactose) content. Adding sugar to other foods such as cereals is unnecessary.
5 Protein-calorie malnutrition, or PCM, is suffered by children in countries where drought or torrential rain ruins the crops, or where political strife robs the people of their land.
6 Small children find fried foods difficult to digest. Grilling is better as the extra fat drains off in cooking.
7 Children need some fat in their diet, but too much can cause health problems later in life.

Questions

1 **What is meant by 'nutrients'?**
2 **Give the main function of each of the nutrients listed here.**
3 **Name two kinds of animal protein and two kinds of plant protein, and explain their importance in the child's diet.**
4 **Who are 'vegans'? What care must they take with a child's diet?**
5 **Give three reasons why it is not wise to sweeten a baby's cereal.**
6 **Explain why a one-year-old may refuse fried bacon and eggs, though he enjoys boiled ham and poached eggs.**

Nutrition (2)

Vitamins and minerals

These are chemicals essential for the healthy working of the body – making bones grow straight, keeping the correct balance of salts, forming healthy blood cells, and so on. Vitamins and minerals are found in a wide variety of foods and most people have plenty in their diet. However, pregnant mothers (p. 50) and small children have special needs.

1 Children's Vitamin Drops contain vitamins A, C, and D. The other vitamins are found in good supply in human and cow's milk. Vitamin Drops are recommended from one month up to two years, but many children take them up to the age of five. Parents must be careful to give the stated amount; too much vitamin A or D can cause health problems.
2 Nearly all foods sold for infants and toddlers have vitamins added.
3 Vitamin-D Drops and calcium found in cheese and milk must be taken by Asian children to prevent rickets (p. 77).
4 Fresh fruit and vegetables are a rich source of vitamin C, but this can be destroyed in cooking or storing for too long. The fresh food must be plunged into a small amount of boiling water and cooked for a few minutes only.
5 Iron is added to baby formula. After weaning, the child's diet should include iron-rich foods such as liver and meat, to prevent anaemia (p. 50).
6 Salt should not be added to a child's diet as there is enough in ordinary food. Too much salt causes health problems later in life.

Vitamins in the body	
Vitamins	*Best foods*
A (can be stored in the liver)	Fish-liver oils, sardines, liver, milk and butter, fresh green vegetables
B_1 (cannot be stored)	Yeast, wheat germ, egg yolk, liver, soya beans
B_2 and other B vitamins	Yeast, milk, cheese, kidneys, peanuts, meat, poultry
C (lost by over-cooking or storing)	Citrus fruits, tomatoes, onions, pineapples, berries, green vegetables
D (can be made in skin in sunlight and stored)	Fish-liver oils, eggs, liver, milk
E	Green vegetables, wheat germ, milk
K (stored in liver)	Dark-green leafy vegetables (found in most foods)

Dietary fibre

This is the tough part of food from plants – the stringy parts of celery, string beans, oranges, and bran in wholemeal bread. Plant fibre cannot be digested. It is important in the diet to help the muscles push the waste food out of the body.

Foods rich in dietary fibre.

A balanced diet

Parents do not have to be experts in diet sheets, nor do they have to count up calories or follow charts. But everyone dealing with small children should have some knowledge of food values. A mixed diet means eating a wide variety of foods – not sticking to one special favourite. This makes sure the body gets all the nutrients it needs: the child is having a balanced diet.

A balanced diet consists of:

1. *Kilojoules* (or Calories) in sufficient quantity.
2. *Protein* for growth, body-building, cell replacement.
3. *Carbohydrate* for energy.
4. *Fat* for energy, heat and food storage.
5. *Vitamins* for healthy growth and development.
6. *Minerals* for healthy growth and development.
7. *Water* for transport and healthy working of the body.
8. *Dietary fibre* for help in getting rid of waste food.

Suggestions for a typical toddler's menu

Breakfast	*Lunch*	*Tea*
Cereal with milk	Minced meat	Sardines or pilchards on toast,
Egg, boiled or poached	Mashed potato	or cheese on toast,
	Carrots, beans	or marmite and cress sandwiches
Brown bread and butter	Tinned pears	Junket, yoghurt and
	Mug of milk	blackcurrant sauce
Fresh fruit juice		Celery to chew
		Mug of hot milk,
		or cocoa with cake or biscuit

Questions

1. **Write down the ages when vitamin drops are recommended.**
2. **What foods contain vitamin C? Give instructions on how to cook them.**
3. **What advice would you give about (a) iron and (b) salt in a child's diet?**
4. **What is dietary fibre? Explain its function in the body.**
5. **Copy out and learn what a balanced diet consists of.**

Feeding problems and obesity

In a recent study, newly-weaned babies were allowed to feed themselves from a wide variety of wholesome foods: milk, eggs, fruit, vegetables, wholegrain cereals, and so on. They loved it. They used fingers, trying a bit from each dish until they decided which dishes they liked best. When their meals were studied, the research people found each baby had balanced his diet perfectly.

1 Babies have a good sense about how much they need to eat, and what kinds of food they need.
2 Toddlers have certain likes and dislikes – sudden crazes and sudden hates – which change from time to time.
3 New babies need lots of feeds because they are growing quickly. Toddlers do not eat much; they have quite small appetites.

What are 'feeding problems'?

Babies scream urgently for food: parents react with urgency to supply it. This sense of food being needed so urgently by the baby goes on in the parent long after the child has grown out of his early hungers. Parents beg, plead, and coax the child to eat. They even scoop and force back food which the child has spat out. At first, the child may eat more because he likes all the fuss. Later, he begins to think of meal times as battles (which they are!), and refuses everything he senses parents are especially keen for him to eat.

1 A baby should not be forced or coaxed to eat. He will not starve.
2 He has a natural appetite which changes as he changes.
3 Unwanted food should be removed without any fuss by parents.
4 Interfering with a child's natural appetite causes feeding problems.

Obesity

It is likely the notion of a 'bonny' (fat) baby comes from the days when there was not enough food. If a baby was fat, it meant the parents were successful. Nowadays, a fat baby is called obese, not bonny.

When extra food is eaten, it is stored in fat cells under the skin. The baby makes these fat cells during the first year of life. A fat baby makes far more than a slim baby – when the fat person grows up he has problems with weight. He cannot diet easily because of the extra fat cells waiting to be filled up. A fat adult risks heart disease, and other illnesses.

Points to consider

1 A baby on formula milk should not be forced to finish the contents of his bottle if he does not seem to want to.
2 At weaning, it is better to start the baby on protein foods such as beef broth than to add fattening cereal or sugar to milk.
3 A hungry child does not need fattening snacks of biscuits or crisps. A stick of raw celery or carrot, a slice of apple or orange can be given instead.
4 It is better not to associate food with reward. An unhappy child may overeat simply to get parents' praise.
5 A child can start feeding himself very early. Table manners come later, when the child wants to show how grown-up and clean he can be.
6 A child with a normal appetite who suddenly stops eating is ill. Take him to the doctor or clinic.
7 It is sad to think of feeding problems and obesity in industrialized countries, when half the world's babies go to bed hungry every night.

A mother tries to force her well-fed child to eat; while in Namalu, Uganda, a mother watches over her starving child.

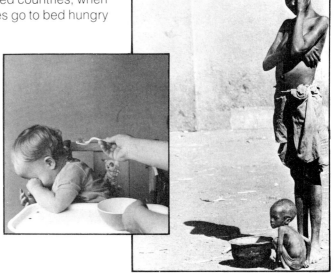

Questions

1 **What did the research people learn when they let babies feed themselves?**
2 **Why do new babies need lots of feeds?**
3 **In your own words, explain how feeding problems usually start.**
4 **What advice would you give a parent who worried his child was not eating enough?**
5 **What is meant by 'obesity'?**
6 **Explain why a fat adult has problems when he tries to lose weight.**
7 **In your own words, explain why it is better not to associate food with reward.**

Elimination

When the nutrients have been used, there is waste matter left over. Waste liquid is called urine. Waste solids are called faeces. Getting rid of waste is called elimination (opening the bowels, passing water). A baby has no control over these actions until about twenty months, often later. A small baby put on a pot may 'oblige': it is luck, not training.

Equipment

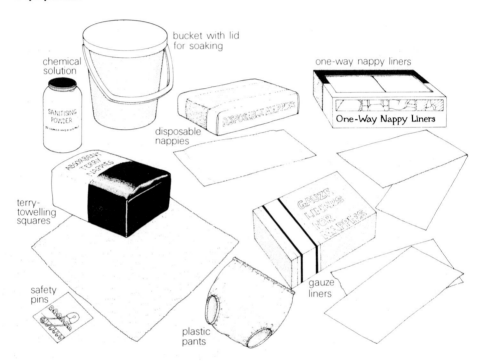

bucket with lid for soaking

chemical solution

SANITISING POWDER

one-way nappy liners

One-Way Nappy Liners

disposable nappies

DISPOSABLE NAPPIES

terry-towelling squares

ABSORBENT TERRY NAPPIES

GAUZE LINERS FOR NAPPIES

gauze liners

safety pins

plastic pants

1 Small babies are usually changed after each feed.
2 An older baby needs more frequent changes because (a) there is more urine, (b) a soaking nappy gets cold once the baby is crawling around.
3 A strong smell of ammonia only happens when there are faeces and urine in the nappy: germs in the faeces cause the urine to smell high.
4 A baby's bottom gets sore from too much washing: wipe with damp cotton-wool, pat dry, put on barrier creams such as zinc and castor oil cream.
5 Nappies must be thoroughly cleaned, thoroughly rinsed, thoroughly dried.
6 Detergents irritate a baby's delicate skin. Soft soap powders should be used for washing nappies; two tablespoons of vinegar added to the wash stops the ammonia forming.

Pot training

Sometime during the second year, the toddler clutches himself or makes urgent signals – parents rush for the pot. They praise his efforts: they do not tell him off if it is too late. Once a toddler's mind has developed enough for him to 'pay attention' to the connection between the pot and his need to use it, parents can begin their training. Nappies can be left off during the day – the pot is kept close by. Each time the toddler succeeds, he is praised. When he fails, the mess is calmly cleared up and ignored. Within a week, the toddler will be clean and dry during the day. This method works if the child is not made to feel anxious when he fails. Any sort of pressure from parents (scolding, looking upset or disappointed) gets in the way of the toddler's subtle learning about his inner feelings and the pot. A tensed, shamed toddler 'pays attention' to parents' pressure instead of the feelings which come when he needs to use the pot.

Points to consider

1   Any feelings of disgust parents have about elimination are automatically picked up by the child.
2   Many one-year-olds like to play with faeces. Parents frown to show this is not acceptable behaviour, but they do not make the child feel 'dirty' or 'bad'.
3   Calm smiling parents can expect pot training to be over in a week.
4   Forcing a child to stay on the pot makes him stubborn; or anxious.
5   Adults have to remember that only the child can learn for himself the connection between inner feelings and the need to use the pot.
6   Praising successes and ignoring failures leaves the child's mind clear to concentrate on what he is learning.

Things do not always go smoothly

The three-year-old is usually clean and dry by day, and at night. But upset feelings can change this. (Even some adults fear they may wet themselves under extreme excitement.) A child who suddenly begins wetting or soiling again must not be told off. Parents need to discover the real cause of his distress: the new baby, starting school, illness, and so on. Once the child's upset feelings are put right, the problem of losing control just vanishes.

The medical name for bed-wetting in an older child is enuresis. Again, parents must be calm and understanding. It helps if they remember that the condition will eventually stop. Teenagers do not wear nappies. A child who goes on wetting the bed after the age of four should be taken to the doctor in case there is something physically wrong.

Questions

1   **What are the names for (a) waste liquid and (b) waste solids?**
2   **What is meant by 'elimination'?**
3   **In your own words, explain why strict hygiene is necessary in the care of nappies.**
4   **Write a short essay describing what you would do so that pot training was over within a week.**
5   **What should parents do if a three and a half-year-old child suddenly started wetting again?**

Teeth and bones

Teeth

Milk teeth are already formed in the jaw of a new-born baby. They begin to appear at six months. There are twenty in all: the biting teeth at the front, the tearing and grinding teeth at the sides and back. The mother starts caring for her baby's teeth during pregnancy when she makes sure her diet is rich in calcium foods such as cheese and milk, and vitamins A, C, and D. These foods are also necessary for the development of strong bones. It is very important to look after milk teeth so that the permanent teeth which appear later come down in the right place.

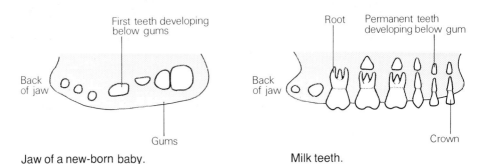

Jaw of a new-born baby.   Milk teeth.

Care of the milk teeth

1   When teeth first appear, they and the gums should be cleaned with a dab of fluoride toothpaste on a piece of gauze.
2   A soft bristle toothbrush can be used by one year. Later, the child is taught to brush up and down to get rid of food caught between the teeth.
3   A child needs to visit the dentist at two for his first check-up. Waiting until there is toothache means waiting until the decay is quite advanced.
4   Soft sugary foods leave a deposit of plaque which allows germs to breed and cause decay. This is called dental caries.
5   After sweets and school lunches, the child should chew an apple or raw carrot. This keeps the gums healthy and cleans away the sticky plaque.
6   Teeth must be thoroughly cleaned night and morning. At an early age a child can develop habits of hygiene which last throughout life.

Bones

A baby's bones are soft and bendy. They harden slowly as the child grows. The fontanelle or soft spot is a diamond-shaped gap on the top of the baby's skull. It allows room for growing and is closed by the first birthday. There is a much smaller fontanelle at the back of the baby's skull. Toddlers look bow-legged when they begin walking. They should not have too much bulky nappy between their legs. Between three and seven, the child may look knock-kneed. Neither bow legs nor knock knees are to be worried about as they disappear by the time the child is eight or nine. The disease, rickets, has been discussed in the section on mother's and baby's diet (p. 77).

Feet

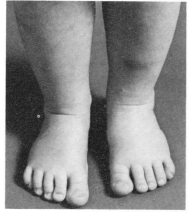 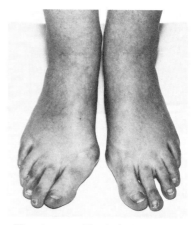

The perfect feet of a two-year-old child.   The damaged feet of a teenager.

Babies have perfect feet, with a little pad of fat on each instep. By the time they are teenagers, many have lost their smooth straight toes, and developed painful corns and bunions. The soft bones in a child's foot can be easily deformed (twisted out of shape) unless great care is taken throughout childhood.

Points to consider

1 A small child should run barefoot whenever this is possible.
2 'Stretch' socks which do not really stretch cramp the toes together and deform soft bones. Nylon socks should not be used. Cotton or wool mixtures are best.
3 Shoes must fit snugly round the heel and have a strap over the instep to hold the foot firmly, and give it proper support.
4 Socks and shoes need to be at least a half-size larger than the child's feet to allow the growing toes room to lie flat.
5 Foot measures must be used before buying new shoes. Flexible good quality leather shoes are expensive, but well worth the extra money.
6 Little girls may crave for fashionable shoes. Parents should not give in unless they are well-fitting and comfortable too; most are not.
7 Standing still is more difficult than walking or running. Small children cannot stand still, and should not be expected to do so.

Questions

1 **When do the first milk teeth usually appear?**
2 **Why is it important to look after milk teeth? How many are there?**
3 **At what age should a child first visit the dentist? Why?**
4 **Which foods encourage germs? Which help the child's mouth stay clean?**
5 **Name four foods which are essential for the health of teeth and bones.**
6 **What are the fontanelles? When do they close up?**
7 **In what way can something as harmless as a sock cause deformity?**
8 **Name two things to look for when buying shoes for a small child.**

Temperature control

Body heat comes from the chemical changes in the body which go on all the time; it comes from movement and exercise. The average body temperature is about 37°C. Babies have higher body temperatures, old people lower ones. Body heat stays the same, except during illness. There is a mechanism which keeps the body temperature constant. This is not switched on in small babies. They cannot control their body heat.

1 A warmly-fed, warmly-dressed and well-covered baby will stay warm as long as the room temperature does not drop below about 20°C.
2 It is no use putting extra blankets on an already cold baby: once he is cold he stays cold; he cannot warm himself up.
3 Extra blankets are only useful to keep in body heat which is already there.

Hypothermia

A cold baby quickly becomes dangerously ill. He lies heavy and still; he may not be interested in food. Hands and feet swell. The skin feels cold to touch. This condition is known as hypothermia (below body temperature). Medical help is needed urgently, so that the baby can be heated slowly and safely. Old people also suffer from hypothermia.

Over-heating

1 In warm climates or hot weather, care needs to be taken so a baby does not become too hot.
2 A baby who is too hot sweats; tiny beads of moisture appear on the skin,
3 Sweat helps to cool him down, but only if he is not over-dressed.
4 Nylon and plastic materials trap in heat and stop the sweat evaporating.
5 Too many layers of wool may cause prickly heat and itchy reddened skin.
6 Cotton is a good absorber of sweat and allows air to move freely.

Learning to read a thermometer

At first, it is not easy to read a thermometer. It needs to be turned slowly till the dark bar can be seen. Check where the small marking for the average temperature is (usually an arrow). Always hold the thermometer at the glass end. A sharp flick of the wrist will shake down the mercury. Learning to read a thermometer takes quite a bit of practice; keep trying on yourself until you can do it quickly, and with confidence.

Taking a baby's temperature

1 Wipe the bulb end clean with cotton wool and check the mercury is down.
2 Pick the baby up gently. Sit with him held comfortably in your arms.

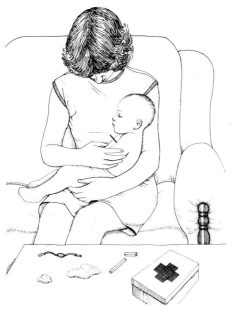

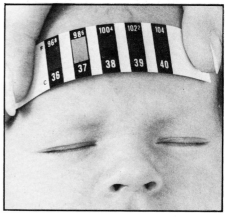

This is a new, simpler way of taking a baby's temperature. It is called the Feverscan. The strips change colour to indicate the level of body heat.

3 Tuck the thermometer right up so the bulb end is snug against his armpit.
4 Hold the baby's arm still for three minutes; croon or chat quietly to him.
5 Remove the thermometer gently. Place the baby back in the cot, then read the temperature.
6 Write down what it is, shake the mercury down, then wipe the bulb end clean and return the thermometer to the first aid box.
7 Do not take a child's temperature unless he seems feverish (very hot, restless, ill). It is not necessary for colds, tummy upsets, minor aches.
8 Never leave a child alone with a thermometer. He may chew the broken glass or swallow the poisonous mercury – or both!
9 Do not take a temperature after a hot bath, or hot drink. The reading will be falsely high.

Questions

1 **What is the average body temperature?**
2 **Name two groups of people with lower and higher body temperatures.**
3 **A baby should never be undressed in a freezing cold room. Explain why.**
4 **Describe the signs and symptoms of hypothermia.**
5 **In your own words, explain why extra blankets will not warm a baby who is already cold.**
6 **Name two fabrics you would not use in a very hot climate. Give reasons why they are unsuitable.**
7 **Why do you think it necessary to write down the temperature?**
8 **Why should you never leave a child alone with a thermometer?**

Infectious childhood diseases

1 Whooping cough

Incubation time: 7–10 days

Symptoms begin with a cold and hacking cough. The cough gets worse as the temperature rises. The cough comes so suddenly the child has no time to draw breath. The 'whoop' sound made by older children is caused by quick breaths taken between the spasms. The coughing gets so violent it is often followed by vomiting. Small babies cannot whoop; their faces turn blue from lack of breath. It is an extremely distressing disease but it can be prevented by immunization (p. 96).

Treatment　Call the doctor. She will prescribe antibiotics (bacteria killers) to prevent complications such as pneumonia. Food lost by vomiting must be replaced. Milky meals such as junkets are soothing. Frequent sips of fresh juice and water replace lost fluid and vitamin C. Keep the child in bed until his temperature drops, then let him have plenty of fresh air if it is warm, or give him breathing exercises indoors. Whooping cough may last about three weeks, but it takes much longer for the child to regain full health and strength.

2 Chicken pox

Incubation time: 10 days

Symptoms begin with a mild cold and a rise in temperature. The rash appears in the next twenty-four hours. Red raised spots show up on the chest, stomach and back. They spread to the face, and the arms and legs. Each spot turns into a watery blister, which dries up and forms into a very itchy crust. If the blisters appear in the mouth, they make swallowing very painful. However, it is a mild disease. Most children have it before the age of ten.

Treatment　Keep in bed until the temperature goes down. Calamine lotion dabbed on the spots relieves the itching. If the child scratches the drying crusts, a little 'pox' mark stays as a permanent scar. An older child may enjoy

dabbing his spots and can be told the reason why he must not pick at them. Cut the nails of a younger child and tuck his hands in cotton gloves. Exciting stories and fun games will help distract his attention. Chicken pox is a mild illness. The child is completely recovered in two weeks.

2 Rubella (German measles)

Incubation time: 10–21 days
Symptoms begin with a slight temperature and the outbreak of pink spots. The spots are small and flat, and cover the body for about two days only. Glands at the back of the neck may become sore and swollen, but this is not usual. It is such a mild disease no treatment is needed. The child does not feel unwell. However, the child must be kept away from pregnant women (p. 47). It is important girls have rubella before puberty.

4 Measles

Incubation time: 7–10 days
Symptoms begin with a temperature, running eyes and nose, and a sore throat. The symptoms get worse; a high fever, hacking cough, very sore eyes, and a miserably distressed child. It is almost a relief when the blotchy dark red spots begin to appear. A child with measles is quite ill, and needs good nursing to prevent complications.
Treatment   Call the doctor. Keep the child in bed until the temperature drops. The room should be dark and quiet; light and noise are hurtful. Tempting snacks are needed, with plenty of milk, orange juice, and sips of water. The rash fades and the temperature falls in about five days. The child is usually well after two weeks. Measles is such a nasty disease that parents should make sure their child is immunized against it (p. 96).

5 Mumps

Incubation time: 2–3 weeks
Symptoms begin with slight fever and sore throat, also swellings on the sides of the cheek in front of the ear. These give the face the 'mumps' look, and it is painful to open the mouth.
Treatment   Keep the child in bed until the temperature drops. A soft diet is needed as the child will not chew, and plenty of fluids. It is a mild illness and the child is quite well in two weeks. However, there may be complications in older boys if the testicles feel tender, which could affect their fertility. In very rare cases, a girl's ovaries may be affected. It is good to have mumps before puberty.

Questions

1 **Which of the infectious diseases require a call to the doctor?**
2 **Write about the symptoms and treatment of chicken pox.**
3 **Which of the infectious diseases should (a) a girl and (b) a boy catch before puberty? Give reasons for your answer.**
4 **Describe the treatment for measles.**

Nursing a sick child

Babies can run alarmingly high temperatures, especially in the evenings. Knowing this stops parents becoming too frightened. If they cool the baby down, there is a chance his temperature will be normal the next morning. If it is still high, the doctor must be called. She will need to be told both temperatures, and the signs of illness parents have noticed. The doctor should be called at nine in the morning, ten at the latest if a home visit is necessary.

Cooling a baby down

1　The baby is undressed, and tepid – not cold – water is sponged over his hot burning skin for a few minutes.
2　The tepid water evaporates from the baby's skin, causing cooling.
3　The baby is patted dry, dressed in an absorbent cotton nightgown, returned to his cot, and covered with a light absorbent blanket.
4　Tepid sponging brings the temperature down, making the baby comfortable enough to get some sleep.

A very sick child

1　He needs the comfort of his bed, in a warm, dark, quiet room.
2　When he wakes and is restless, he needs the comfort of his parents.
3　Strict care must be taken with his medicine. No extra spoonfuls should be added.
4　He needs plenty of fluids: milk, fruit juices, fizzy drinks – not food.
5　He needs reassurance. 'Are you feeling better, pet?' is more positive than 'I can't bear seeing you so ill, my poor darling.'

A slightly ill child

1　He needs equal amounts of company and peaceful times.
2　Left alone in his room, he becomes fretful, whining and demanding.
3　He will be happier tucked on the sofa, playing simple games, watching television, drifting off to sleep when he feels tired.
4　He will need 'babying' until the miseries of being ill have passed.

Going to hospital

Unlike visits to the dentist, many children do not have to go to hospital. But it is better if a child has some idea of what hospitals are for – just in case. This is why parents encourage children to play doctors and nurses with toy medical equipment, and read stories about children going to hospital. But it is always a frightening experience in reality. Parents should do their best to stay with a child during the separation anxiety stage (p. 148). If they cannot, they should visit frequently and stay as long as possible.

Points to consider

1   If treatment is likely to be painful, a child should be told that doctors and nurses will be as gentle as they can.
2   An older child may understand that treatment will get him better. A younger child needs exciting distractions to keep his mind free from fear.
3   All children need to take familiar and beloved toys with them for comfort. Listening to stories about home life is very reassuring too.
4   Gifts do not spoil a sick child. He needs a great deal of fuss, and a great deal of extra love and attention.
5   Parents must turn up when they have promised a visit. They should not slip away when the child is opening his presents. Either of these things will make the child feel abandoned.
6   All children regress during illness. Parents can expect babyish behaviour from a sick child for quite a while after he returns home.

Questions

1   **What advice would you give a parent whose baby runs a high temperature in the evening?**
2   **Explain how to cool a baby down, and what good effects this has.**
3   **Name four things a very sick child needs.**
4   **Write a short paragraph explaining why it is more helpful to ask a child if he feels better than to be too sympathetic.**
5   **Write a short account of how you would prepare a sick child for going to hospital.**

Immunization

A baby is protected against terrible diseases such as polio, diphtheria, and tetanus, by having shots of very weak or dead germs. Over a period of time, his body builds up defences against the diseases. The shots are spaced out so the baby's only reactions are a bit of grizzling, and a tender spot which vanishes in a few days. Booster shots are given as the child gets older, to make certain he stays immune from the diseases.

Average times for immunization

1 The 'triple' vaccine against diphtheria, whooping cough, and tetanus, is given at three, five, and nine months of age. The booster shot is given at the age of five.
2 The polio vaccine is given at the same time, though not by injection. It is given as a syrup to babies, and on a lump of sugar to an older child.
3 A booster dose of tetanus and polio vaccine is offered when the person leaves school.
4 The vaccine against measles is given during the child's second year.
5 The rubella (German measles) vaccine is offered to girls between 11 and 13 (before puberty). The disease is very mild in young children, but very dangerous in pregnancy to the development of the unborn baby.
6 The BCG vaccine against tuberculosis is given between 11 and 13 to both sexes, but only if a skin test shows it might be necessary.

Contra-indications

'Contra' means against. A contra-indication is a sign that the baby should not have a particular vaccine. Things like eczema (skin disease), epilepsy (fits), or really bad effects after a previous immunization are taken into account. There is great argument over the whooping-cough vaccine. It causes brain damage in one out of every 300,000 children. But the disease itself is so horrible that many parents decide to take the small risk. (It is likely that medical research will soon be able to make the vaccine completely safe.)

Questions

1 **Average times for immunization vary from country to country. The UK average is given here. Copy it out and learn it if it is the same as in your country. If not, copy out the list suitable for 'your' children.**
2 **Find out what immunizations are needed in one equatorial country of your choice.**

First aid

The first-aid box

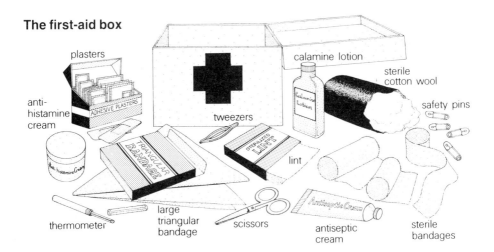

plasters · calamine lotion · sterile cotton wool · anti-histamine cream · tweezers · safety pins · TRIANGULAR BANDAGE · STERILIZED LINT · lint · thermometer · large triangular bandage · scissors · antiseptic cream · sterile bandages

As well as the items shown in the picture, the first-aid box should contain:
(a) family doctor's telephone number, pad and pencil for writing down instructions, correct change for a call-box if there is no home telephone.
(b) telephone numbers of health visitor, social worker, child health centre, for advice on simple health or social problems.
(c) address of the nearest hospital with a twenty-four hour accident and emergency department.
(d) address and telephone number of nearest grandparent, friend, neighbour, who will look after other children in an emergency.
The first-aid box should have a child-proof lock, or be kept in a locked cupboard.

Cuts, bruises, and minor accidents

1 Dirt must be gently washed out of cuts.
2 Bleeding fingers are held upwards under the cold running tap.
3 Tiny splinters of wood or glass must be removed with fine tweezers.
4 Grit in the eye is removed with the edge of a clean tissue, after rolling the eyelid back to find its exact position.
5 A nose bleed can be stopped by sitting the child upright and pinching the bridge of his nose for five to ten minutes.
6 Bruises can be admired – 'what a whopper!' – or dabbed with cold pads.
7 Many small cuts heal better if left open to the air. But plasters have a therapeutic effect for some children: they believe in the 'magic' of a plaster and immediately feel better.
8 Children can be more frightened by the unexpectedness of a knock than by the pain it causes. Many minor accidents only need 'kisses all better' to restore confidence.

Questions

1 **How would you (a) treat a bleeding finger and (b) stop a nose bleed?**
2 **Copy out the contents of the first-aid box in your book.**

Safety (1)

1 A baby's natural curiosity puts him in danger: investigating the bleach bottle under the sink; standing up in the pram for a better view of the world.
2 The small child is in danger because he can only 'pay attention' to one thing at a time. If the ball runs into the road, he runs after it.
3 He does not deliberately break the traffic rules he has been taught. He cannot 'pay attention' to two different things at the same time.
4 Parents and others in charge of small children have to be their eyes, ears, and mind until they are at least seven years of age.

At home

The kitchen can be a very dangerous place. Cookers, knives, cleaning materials, electrical equipment, are all potential dangers. Mothers and babies spend a lot of time in the kitchen. It must be made as safe as possible.

Traffic

Modern children must be taught to regard traffic in the same way as primitive children regarded wild beasts. This is not easy for parents because a growling tiger is terrifying, whereas parents drive cars and bus rides are fun. It is parents' attitude and example which helps the child most. In the car, a carry-cot is firmly strapped down; there is a safety seat for the toddler; a seat belt for the older child. On the streets, parents do not dash across the road: they walk the child to the crossing and wait, explaining 'look, listen, look again' before they cross. They make sure the outer doors at home are firmly closed, always.

Accident-prone children?

Some children seem to have far more accidents than others. This may be because they are more active and outgoing, so they take greater risks. But the child who is suffering from unhappy emotions is likely to have more accidents. He walks into closed doors or bangs his head on the sharp edges of the furniture, long after he should have learned to stop making these mistakes. He needs his unhappy emotions put right before he can begin to take care of himself in these simple ways.

Parents

Accidents cause anguish in adults – dreadful, guilt-ridden anguish. It is heart-stopping to watch a child balancing on the edge of a high wall. Over-anxious parents risk making their child too timid. Parents have the incredibly difficult task of keeping their child safe while, at the same time, keeping his spirit of adventure alive.

Questions

1 **Explain how a baby's natural curiosity puts him in danger.**
2 **In your own words, explain why a child is not being disobedient when he runs after a ball in the road.**
3 **Who are the people responsible for a small child's safety?**
4 **Give two examples of the ways parents help a child learn road safety.**
5 **List as many dangers as you can in the drawing of the kitchen. How could these dangers be avoided?**
6 **Explain why an outgoing child is likely to have more accidents.**
7 **What should parents check for if their child has the sort of accidents he should have grown out of?**
8 **Write a paragraph sympathizing with parents by explaining how difficult their task of taking safe care of a child can be.**

Safety (2)

Suffocation and choking

Pillows, prop-feeding, and such things as plastic bibs left around the baby's neck after feeding are dangerous. Tiny toys or objects such as beads or large crusts will cause choking. If something does get stuck in the throat, it must be hooked out immediately with the finger. If this fails, turn the child upside down and bang hard on his back.

Poisoning

Dangerous cleaning fluids must be locked away. All medicines must be kept in a child-proof locked cabinet. If poisoning does occur, telephone the doctor, explaining what the child has taken. Follow her instructions.

Burns and scalds

For small burns, hold the damaged part under the cold tap for ten minutes. For large areas, put the child in a bath of tepid water. If the child's clothes are on fire, smother the blaze in a rug, coat, or blanket. This cuts off the oxygen and the fire is extinguished. Give the child small sips of water to replace body fluid which is lost at the site of a burn. Call the doctor.

Falls

Check straps in the pram, high chair, and push-chair. There must be gates at the top of the stairs, and no stools, tables, or chairs near any windows.
After a fall, ring the doctor at once if the child is unconscious for a few seconds or seems drowsy, or if he is sick or has bleeding from the ears. If a bone seems broken, the child must not be moved until the doctor or ambulance arrives. Cover the child with a light blanket but <u>do not</u> give him anything to drink.

Drowning

Never leave a child alone at water-play, in the bath, or paddling pool. If a child is found not breathing, either from suffocation or drowning, he must be given the kiss of life immediately. This is not easy to learn. It should be taught by a properly-trained instructor.

1 Check there is nothing blocking the airway. Put the head far back so that there is a straight passage for air.

2 Take a breath. Seal your lips right over a small child's nose and mouth.

3 Blow gently out, take another breath, blow gently out again.

4 Watch to see if the chest rises. Continue till help arrives, or the child begins breathing on her own.

Dial 999

In all accidents, speed is essential. Shout for a neighbour to dial 999, while first aid is being carried out. If the parent is alone, and has no telephone, she must (a) become expert at first aid by going to classes, and (b) make special arrangements by which she can contact the outside world <u>before</u> the baby is born. Accidents can happen in the most safely-kept homes.

Questions

1 **Name two things which cause suffocation and two which cause choking.**
2 **What should a parent do if the doorbell rings in the middle of bathtime?**
3 **What is the correct treatment for small burns or scalds?**
4 **What should you do if a child's clothes catch fire?**
5 **Name two things a parent who lives in an isolated cottage must do before the birth of the baby.**

Milestones of physical development

A baby develops from the top down. The neck and shoulder muscles must be strong before he can sit, the trunk strong before he can stand. His time clock for development depends more on what he inherits than on his environment; but a baby stuck in a pram will not crawl as soon as a baby sitting on the floor surrounded by interesting-looking objects.

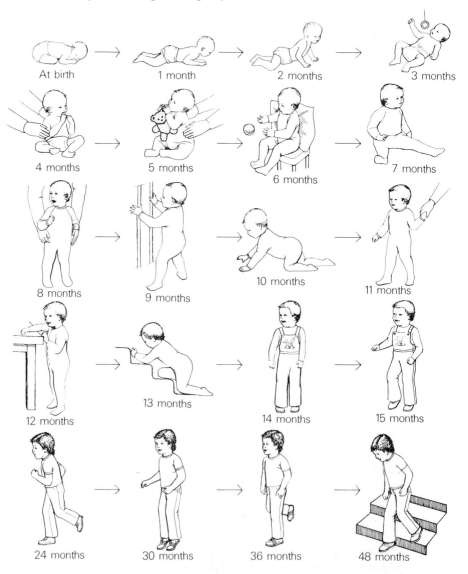

At birth → 1 month → 2 months → 3 months

4 months → 5 months → 6 months → 7 months

8 months → 9 months → 10 months → 11 months

12 months → 13 months → 14 months → 15 months

24 months → 30 months → 36 months → 48 months

1   *Six weeks:* smiles at mother; eyes stare at a ring on string and follow the mother.
2   *Three months:* turns head to sound, head bobs down on mother's shoulder.
3   *Six months:* head steady and back straight when held on shoulder; sits with support of cushions; stretches arms to be lifted up.

4   *Six to twelve months:* develops hand skills, stage by stage.
5   *Seven to nine months:* sits up without support but cannot go into reverse (lie down); may cry with tiredness if this is not understood by parent.
6   *Nine months:* trunk strong enough so he can twist around to toy on either side; sits without support for ten minutes; may pull himself up on furniture.
7   *One year:* standing, walking only with support: gets around by crawling, bottom shuffle, bear walk on hands and feet, cruising.
8   *Thirteen to fifteen months:* walks without support but cannot go into reverse – falls down; creeps up stairs; cannot throw ball without falling over.
9   *Two years:* can manage stairs alone, two feet per step; walks into ball trying to kick it; squats on haunches to rest or examine something, can rise to feet after squatting; sits astride tricycle but cannot use pedals.
10 *Three years:* goes up stairs, one foot per step; down stairs, still two feet per step; usually jumps off bottom step; plays on climbing frame; rides tricycle; stands for brief moment on one foot only.
11 *Four years:* goes down stairs, one foot per step; runs on tiptoe; climbs ladders, hops on one foot; stand on one foot for three to five seconds.
12 *Five years:* skips, dances, hops; stands on one foot for eight to ten seconds; very skilful at using all the equipment in the playground.

It may be useful here to re-read the section on 'Averages, individuals, milestones' (pp. 68–69).

Parents put a great deal of importance on milestones of physical development. They are enormously proud of 'early' sitting unaided, of 'early' walking. They may be puzzled when the health visitor wants their child to play with bricks, or asks him questions about his name, and so on. She does not seem much interested in how 'clever' he is to be sitting up.

But the health visitor knows there is a wide variation in developing physical skills. If the baby is healthy, he will develop these skills at the right time for him. She is looking for the more subtle signs of other kinds of development: does the baby look alert? will he smile readily? how many words can he say? how are his manipulative (hand) skills progressing?

Parents are right to be proud of every new skill their child develops. But is it more 'clever' to be walking, or to be talking at two years?

Questions

1   **Name two things a baby can do at six weeks.**
2   **Would you expect a baby to sit unaided at six months?**
3   **Some babies never crawl. They go straight from bottom-shuffling to walking. Does this matter at all?**
4   **Name two methods of travel in a one-year-old.**
5   **Describe the way a child goes up and down stairs between the ages of two and four.**
6   **How long can you stand on one foot for? Write down how long a child can do this between the ages of three and five.**

Further work on Chapter 4

1   Study children up to the age of seven, whenever and wherever possible. Make detailed notes of what you observe, with special reference to the children's physical development. Places to visit include child health clinics, crèches, mother and toddler clubs, pre-school playgroups, nursery schools, adventure playgrounds, parks, infant schools.

2   Do a full project on the advantages and disadvantages of both breast- and bottle-feeding. The local health education officer or health visitor may be able to arrange a demonstration of breast-feeding.

3   Make up a baby's bottle from formula milk. Write notes on (a) correct concentration and (b) strict hygiene in preparation.

4   Find out about the scandal of selling dried formula milk to mothers in under-developed countries. Do a full project on this.

5   Prepare and cook a meal for a three-year-old. Write details of the foods you selected, their nutritional values, the way you cooked them.

6   Do a study of the different kinds of nappies available, explaining which sort you would choose, and why.

7   Make an interesting brightly-coloured chart to encourage a pre-school child in dental hygiene.

8   Do a project on children's footwear. A chiropodist from your local clinic may be able to give a talk on this subject.

9   Do a project on either (a) immunization or (b) preparing a child for hospital. Write to the National Association for the Welfare of Children in Hospital for further information.

10   Write to the Royal Society for the Prevention of Accidents for information on a project on safety in the home, including notes on firework parties.

11   If possible, visit a nursery. Make notes on the physical skills of children at different ages.

12   (a)   List six important needs of a baby during the first six months of life.
      (b)   Choose three of these needs and write a paragraph about each to explain how it may be satisfied. (EAEB)

13   Imagine a four-year-old child is coming to stay with you and your family. Describe how and why you would provide him with a balanced nutritional diet.
      How might the diet of a child coming to live in Britain from a hot climate be deficient? Suggest ways of overcoming this. (SUJB)

14   A child's good health depends on a number of factors.
      (a)   State four of these factors and describe how each of them may be provided.
      (b)   During illness, children need special care. State three ways in which you would care for a child under each of the following headings:
            (i)   Cleanliness and comfort
            (ii)   Diet
            (iii)   Giving medicine
            (iv)   Toys and companionship (EMREB)

Chapter 5

Mental health: development of the mind

Nature or nurture?

'Nature' means the things a child inherits from his parents, such as hair colour, general intelligence, a certain kind of temperament. 'Nurture' means the things a child gets from his environment (parents and home) such as a good diet, gentle teaching, company, and love. People argue with great passion over which affects the child most.

A true story

A social worker visiting an isolated farm in America in 1938 found a child hidden away in an attic. She was a six-year-old girl, Anna. Her diet was cow's milk, her living conditions were filthy, she showed signs of starvation. She had been hidden away since she was five and a half months old. Anna was not able to talk, or walk. She could not even make signs to show what she wanted. At the children's home where she was cared for, it took her eighteen months to learn to walk. But she did not learn to talk. Anna died of liver disease when she was ten.

Other children have been found living in the wild. They too were not able to talk. They found it difficult to be friendly with the people who tried to care for them. They were not able to catch up with children of their own age brought up in normal homes. Not one of them lived past puberty.

The girl in this picture is called Kamala. She and her sister Amala were found in a village in India in 1920. They were said to have been brought up by wolves. They were unable to speak.

1   It seems that a child cannot develop well unless he is with other people, no matter what he inherits.
2   It has been shown that strong emotional relationships, especially with the mother, develop during the fairly short time from about six to twenty-four months.
3   Skills such as walking and talking are learned by children throughout the world at roughly the same age, before the second birthday.
4   If a child has not learned to speak at all by the time he is five, it is very unlikely he will ever develop normal speech.

Early learning

It seems there is a 'best' time for learning, and this time is during the first years of life. Later learning can happen, but it is slow and very difficult. As many children are raised in homes where there is no time for this early learning, the nature/nurture argument cannot be proved either way. For example, if a child inherits genes for being clever, it is unlikely he will learn much if he spends all day strapped in his pram and ignored by adults. He cannot teach himself about his world. In the same way, a child cannot develop strong emotional relationships unless there are loving adults near so he can grow attached to them.

Improvements in child care

Over the past fifty years, there has been a revolution throughout the industrialized countries in the standard of physical care. Today's children are taller and stronger; they are healthier, they mature earlier. Physically, most children are very well cared for.

In spite of various education acts and free schooling, the same is not true of the child's mental or emotional development. The cognitive (learning) and affective (feeling) sides of his nature have not kept pace with his improved physical development. Better schooling has not been the answer.

It is thought that some people do not begin to fulfil their potential (whatever abilities they may have inherited). Until quite recently, little was known about a child's mental and emotional needs. Nowadays, it is accepted that a child's personality, the cognitive and affective sides of his nature, is formed in early childhood, long before he goes to school. Nurture is now seen to be concerned with caring for the child's mind and emotions, as well as looking after his bodily needs.

Questions

1 **Explain what is meant by 'nature'.**
2 **Explain what is meant by 'nurture'.**
3 **What seems to be the 'best' time for learning?**
4 **Name two things a child has learned by his second birthday.**
5 **What is meant by the 'cognitive' and the 'affective' sides of a child's nature?**
6 **What is nurture now seen to be concerned with?**

The beginning of learning

The new-born baby can do certain things without thinking such as sucking and swallowing and blinking against a harsh light. These are reflex actions (unlearned) and they help him survive.

But he has to learn practically everything else: to crawl, to clap hands, to talk, and so on. It is not a question of waiting till his muscles and bones are strong enough – remember Anna (p. 106). Anything he wants to do must be learned; bit by bit, day by day, right from the very beginning.

The brain

From the last weeks before birth and up to about the age of six, the brain grows very rapidly. By six, a child's brain has grown to 90% of its adult weight. 90%! During this big spurt in brain growth, the child is cramming in more learning more quickly than he will ever do again. He crams it into his 'mind'.

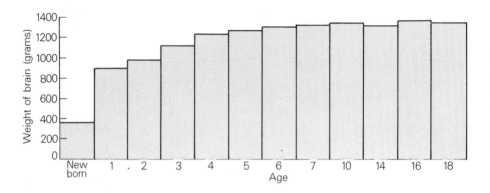

The mind

The 'mind' cannot be seen by cutting open a brain. Though it is now known which parts of the brain control thinking and feeling, it is still not fully understood exactly what the mind is. The words 'mind' and 'brain' are used to stand for the same thing, which they are – in a way. But the brain can be seen as a large object made up of nerve cells. The mind cannot be seen in this way. Who can see thought, memory, imagination, passion? Nevertheless, everyone knows what a mind is. The word 'psychological' is used to refer to the working of the mind and the emotions.

Learning

1 A baby learns by looking, listening, touching, smelling, tasting.
2 He uses all of his five senses to get the information he needs.
3 His mouth is important: he learns the feel of things by licking and sucking. 'Mouthing' slows down by the time the child is one year old.
4 Until then, anything is likely to be mouthed – parents must watch out!
5 A good test for a toy during the first year of life is whether it is clean and safe enough to be sucked, and large enough not to be swallowed.

Keen to learn

The more a baby learns, the keener he is to learn more. When he has learned to grasp for a toy, he will want to learn how to crawl to fetch another one. And as crawling is a slow way to get about, he starts learning to walk . . . and so on. Learning is very exciting. The child is born curious, with a lively inquisitive mind.

Perceptual learning

1   During the first two years, the baby learns mainly by perception. In its simplest form, this means learning by information coming through the senses.
2   He explores people and things – he learns not only what <u>they</u> do to him, but what <u>he</u> can do to them.
3   He is not able to reason things out in his mind. He takes the world as he perceives it, liking some bits and disliking others.

One-year-old Zoe smacks her spoon down onto her cereal. She perceives the lovely squirty spray of food and the lovely splat of noise. She also perceives that a parent does not exactly share her delight! She does not like the parent's frown, but she cannot work out the reason for it. She is likely to make a louder splat because the first was such fun.

Perceptual learning and behaviour

At this early stage of perceptual thinking, it is not possible for a child to be 'naughty'. Naughtiness implies an intention to do wrong. Though Zoe intends to smack her spoon down again, she does not intend to annoy. It is important parents understand this; they can forget about fears of naughty behaviour until later (p. 166). Parents who worry at this early stage can crush the child's excitement at learning by harsh discipline.

Questions

1   **What big change happens in the brain during the first six years of life?**
2   **Is the change bigger from birth to ten, or from ten to eighteen?**
3   **Name the five senses. What is meant by 'mouthing'?**
4   **Explain how a baby learns by perception.**
5   **Write a short paragraph explaining why it is important parents understand that behaviour during perceptual learning cannot be naughty.**

Paying attention

Mary has not been working. The exams start tomorrow. She stares at the open page of her book, gabbling sentences to herself and chewing the edges of her nails. She feels quite frantic. No matter how hard she tries, the facts will not stick in her memory.

Mary thinks she is studying, but she is not. Her mind is crammed with other thoughts: 'Maybe they won't ask this question. Maybe I should be studying something else. How long is the exam? Will it look too awful if I sneak out early? How I hate exams! I'll wear my charm bracelet for luck. It's a nice bracelet. Oh, there's a bit of nail to chew . . .'

Skills for learning

1 Information is not easily stored in the memory.
2 To learn anything, the human mind must 'pay attention'.
3 The facts have to be studied with full concentration.
4 They have to be repeated, then practised, again and again.
5 Only when the mind really pays attention does the information stay firmly in the memory.

Early learning

A baby begins learning from the moment he is born (some people think learning begins before birth). He learns the sight of his mother, the taste of milk, the feel of clothes. He pays attention to these things because they interest him very much. He does not know what 'mother milk clothes' really mean. But he studies them, for brief moments, with full concentration. They are repeated six to eight times during each 24 hours that pass. In time, he begins to make connections: 'mother milk clothes' make him feel good. He gets excited when he sees them; he pays attention because they are important, and interesting, and fun.

Paying attention

1 The important thing to understand about paying attention is that it is a natural thing babies and small children do.
2 They are naturally curious, but only in things which interest them.
3 They themselves choose which things are worth paying attention to.
4 They cannot be forced; they turn their heads away and ignore what they are not ready to learn.
5 They seem to have good sense about what they are ready to understand, and what is too difficult.
6 They also seem to have good sense about how much time they are able to spend in paying attention.

A small experiment

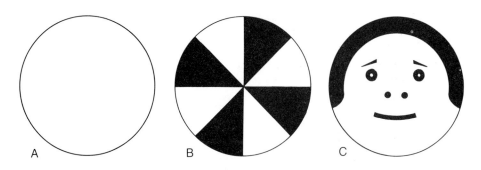

A new-born baby is not interested in these three circles. He may look at them briefly but he is not paying much attention. They do not mean anything (why should they?) so he ignores them.

By the age of four months, he will look at all three. He seems to have learned enough to find them very interesting. He spends longer looking at C than at the other two circles.

By the age of four years, he will be drawing and painting more pictures of C than of A and B.

This small experiment seems to show that the human mind is more interested in faces than in anything else.

Questions

1 **What does 'paying attention' <u>really</u> mean?**
2 **Have you ever felt quite frantic, like Mary? What advice would you give to help her feel better?**
3 **Most people have a 'best' way of studying for an exam. Try to work out your way and explain why it helps you.**
4 **When does a baby begin learning about his world?**
5 **'Mother milk clothes' are repeated six to eight times during one day. Can you guess what is actually happening at those six to eight times?**
6 **Who chooses which things interest a baby: the parent or the infant?**
7 **What might a baby do if a parent tries to force his attention?**
8 **What does the small experiment seem to show?**

Stimulation

'The music was stimulating. It made me get up and dance. I forgot about being shy, and having two left feet.'
'The plot was fascinating. I couldn't stop reading. I had to go on until I found out the ending.'
'It was agony. Now I'm terrified. I'm never going to risk that kind of stimulation again.'

People need stimulation

Stimulation can come from anyone, or anything. It causes a reaction. The right kind of stimulation, as in the first two pictures, drives people forward. The wrong kind of stimulation, as in the third picture, drives the person backward. People need stimulation to light up and keep going their natural urge to learn about life.

The right kind of stimulation

To learn about life, babies must have stimulation too. When they are awake, they need things to satisfy their natural curiosity. Babies like staring at faces, and at brightly-coloured toys. They like listening to rattles, and to gently-spoken words. They do not like sudden violent noise; nor teddy-bears two feet high. Babies are small and cosy; they react best to small and cosy things. By four months, they need toys like plastic cups and teething rings so they can learn how to reach for and grasp with both hands. By the age of one year, toys like wooden spoons, bricks, knocking pegs into holes help the baby learn smooth workings of hands, muscles and eyes.

Not too little – under-stimulation

Some babies are starved of stimulation. They are well-fed and dressed; they are kept warm and clean. But in between bath and feed times, they are left quite alone. They have no company, toys, chats; nothing to stimulate their minds. A baby deprived in this way may cry from loneliness and boredom. Or he may lie quite still, not even bothering to play with his fingers. A baby left alone in his cot will not learn as much as a baby propped in an armchair watching the world around him. He will be backward in learning to smile, to grasp things, to talk, to feed himself – in all the usual things he should have been learning.

Not too much – over-stimulation

Some babies are made anxious and unhappy by too much stimulation. They are given no peace to lie quietly and enjoy a nice day-dream. From the moment they wake, they are picked up and taught . . . and taught . . . and taught. They may even be woken from sleep to show off the newly-learned game of 'pat-a-cake' for the neighbours. Instead of cuddly toys with interesting squeaks, they are given difficult 'educational games' to improve their minds. They grow fretful and anxious, unable to get away from the pressure they are under.

But just right . . .

It is difficult for parents to guess how much stimulation is just right. The baby cannot explain how much he needs; at least, not in words. But he does tell his parents. He tells them by the way he reacts to what is happening. Most parents learn by watching their baby's reactions – which is the common-sense way of learning how anyone feels.

Questions

1 **Copy out the sentence which explains why people need stimulation.**
2 **People react to the same stimulation in different ways. Name three groups of people who would not enjoy very loud pop music.**
3 **Do you think babies need as much stimulation as teenagers? Give as many reasons as you can for your answer.**
4 **'Babies are small and cosy.' Can you name three other things a baby would enjoy, and two other things which might upset him?**
5 **Name two things a baby is learning between the ages of four and twelve months.**
6 **What happens if a baby is starved of stimulation?**
7 **What happens if a baby is given too much stimulation?**
8 **In what ways does a baby 'teach' his parents how much stimulation he needs?**

Learning through play: the first two years

At three months

The baby waves his arms wildly at the bright shiny objects. His movements are jerky; he bangs the rings with his fist. The rings jump and rattle, making lovely dancing patterns. The three-month-old is astonished – and delighted; or so it seems. He bangs again, and again there is exciting noise and movement. Gurgling with pleasure, he bangs the air: nothing happens to the rings. He tries banging them again: he misses and thumps his face instead. Surprised, he stops playing. Then he sees the rings once more. This time he hits right on target; he breaks into delighted grins.

What he is learning

The three-month-old can watch what his fingers are up to. This is called hand and eye co-ordination; hands and eyes working together. But he is not much good at other kinds of co-ordination: muscles and nerves are not developed, hence the wild, jerky, hit-and-miss movements. When he tries banging the rings, he is learning smoother co-ordination. He is also learning about trying to aim for things he wants to touch. He has no idea of 'cause and effect'; but he is setting down patterns of the idea that when he does one thing, he can make another thing happen.

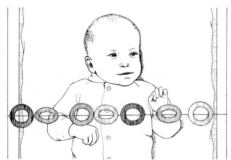
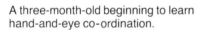

A three-month-old beginning to learn hand-and-eye co-ordination.

A six-month-old beginning to learn manipulative skills.

Manipulative (hand) skills from six to nine months

At six months, the baby cannot let go properly (hand release). He opens his fist and the toy drops away from his grasp.

By seven months, he grasps the bell in both hands: he can pass it from one hand to the other before putting it into his mouth for a better feel.

By eight months he can hold a toy in each hand, though he may seem a bit puzzled as to what to do now both hands are full. He sits sturdily on the floor, surveying his toys: he can easily stretch out and grasp the one he wants to explore next.

By the end of nine months, he has learned the permanence of things: he understands that when toys are out of sight they still exist. Hunting for a half-hidden toy and playing peek-a-boo with parent are popular games.

By the first birthday

The one-year-old is mobile; he can move himself from place to place by crawling, bottom-shuffling, cruising round the room by standing up and holding on to the furniture. This means he will explore anything and everything which catches his attention, from the precious ornament to the dangerous electric flex. He has full hand release, deliberately throwing toys or shopping out of the pram. He peers and points, making bossy calls for them to be returned. His manipulative skills have greatly improved. He can pick up small objects between thumb and first finger in a pincer-like grip.

A one-year-old learning about balance and support.

A two-year-old spends much time practising all these new body skills.

Up until two

From birth to two, the child is in the sensori-motor (sense and movement) stage of development. He learns through his senses (perceptual thinking, p. 107) and he learns through his body movements. There is great joy in being able to stand freely, and then to run around. He spends much time practising these wonderful new body skills.

During the first two years of life the child's play is called 'exploratory', because that is what he is doing – exploring his world.

Questions

1 **What is meant by 'hand and eye' co-ordination and at what age does a baby achieve this?**
2 **A three-month-old makes rather wild jerky movements. Explain why this is.**
3 **What is meant by 'hand release'? At what age does a baby achieve this?**
4 **Name two things an eight-month-old can do with his hands.**
5 **Name a popular game for a nine- to ten-month-old.**
6 **Name three ways in which a one-year-old is mobile.**
7 **Write a paragraph describing the manipulative skills a baby learns in his first year of life.**
8 **Give the correct name for a child's play up until the age of two.**

Learning through play: from two to six

The development of cognitive (thinking) skills

A two-year-old has a concept (general notion) that all animals with legs are dogs. When he meets a cat, he is likely to think it another kind of dog. Over the next few years, he forms the concept that dogs and cats are actually different. He also understands that some four-legged animals are huge and eat grass and are called cows and do not live in people's homes. He then begins to form the concept that there are different classes (groups) of four-legged animals. But he will not be able to explain the difference between a dog and a cow until he is about six.

Concepts are difficult: they have to be thought about quite hard. They include such things as numbers, colours, shapes, sizes, weights, measures, time, space . . . and so on. The child learns these things, quite naturally, through play. At first, he gets them very muddled. He has many misconceptions about his world.

Creative play

Creative play is any kind of play which involves the child in making something. A box of different coloured and different sized bricks, peg boards, nesting beakers, matching shapes are used for learning construction skills. The child gets as much satisfaction from building and fitting things together as he does from dismantling and pulling things apart. The three-year-old in the picture below is learning nearly all of the concepts listed above.

Sand, water, playdough, finger paints, paper and crayons are messy but important parts of creative play. Digging in the sandpit and sloshing water from one carton to another helps the child learn that different things have different properties: water flows, and fills up, and will not stay still, whereas sand has to be lifted, and dumped, and makes a lovely castle. Playdough, or ordinary kitchen dough, is just as exciting as plasticene: wriggly worms and castle walls can be made from the same material. Finger paint, or powder paint mixed with very little water to keep it thick, makes magic patterns at first. Later, the child learns he can make representations of people and things.

Creative play.

Making music with drums, rattling spoons, tinkling triangles, helps the child learn about time, and force of motion, and rhythm. Tin whistles and blowing through combs prepare him for the recorder, and other wind instruments later on. Toy guitars and pianos are popular from about the age of four.

Any form of creative play improves the child's hand-eye co-ordination, his understanding of concepts, his information about the properties of things. He gains concentration and self-control. He experiences one of the great pleasures in life, a sense of achievement.

Imaginative play

At about two, the child is able to use symbols (things which represent other things) in his mind. 'This is my fishing stick,' he says, holding a fork over the plate, imagining the food as little fishes nibbling at his fishing rod. Being able to symbolize things happens at the same time as talking (p. 128); words are representations, too. He enters a fantasy world of make-believe, invention and role-play.

1 About seventy-five per cent of children start imaginative play at two.
2 Invented playmates are common: fifty per cent of only children invent them.
3 Children outgrow invented playmates when they begin school. A child who does not may well be lonely and needing a friend.
4 Role-play turns into proper acting by about five when the child can clearly tell the difference between acting and real life.
5 Imaginative play helps the child act out his inner feelings. If there is a new baby in the family, the child will cradle a doll. If he has been punished, teddy will get punished too.
6 Imaginative play also helps the child learn about different roles: parent, postman, doctor, fireman, bus-lady. He can switch from being one to another in the middle of a game, or he may refuse to answer unless he is called Mr Postman for the whole day.

Imaginative play.

Questions

1 **The author of this book used to believe that dogs were Dads and cats were Mums, and puppies and kittens were boy and girl baby-dogs! Can you remember any misconceptions you had as a very small child?**
2 **In your own words, explain (a) what is meant by a 'concept' and (b) what is meant by a 'misconception'.**
3 **Write a short account of creative play covering (a) what it is, (b) what it helps a child learn, (c) why it is important.**
4 **Write a short account of imaginative play.**

The importance of play

Play is not something small children do to fill up their time. Play is the way all children learn body and mind skills. Play progresses from one stage to the next in a definite time sequence.

A baby in a remote African village discovers his toes as playthings at the same time as a baby in a crowded modern city. A three-year-old African's toys may be different, but he plays at the same stage of development as the city child with 'educational' toys. Play is the natural way children discover themselves and their world.

A child who is ill, or who is very unhappy, stops playing. When he gets better, his level of play is behind that of children of his age. This is because he was not learning while he was not playing. He will catch up in time, but he needs lots of encouragement and praise.

Help with play

Play between people begins very early.

Children do not learn well without help from adults. Their perceptual thinking keeps them repeating the same game unendingly. They need help to take the next step forward. 'Where's it gone?' parents ask, hiding the brick under the plastic cup: a new kind of learning starts. 'Try it this way,' they suggest, tying the thrown-out toy by string to the pram and showing the one-year-old how to haul it back for himself.

When a pile of bricks topples over, a child can see what went wrong. But there are other skills which he cannot judge for himself – such as holding the story book upside down.

Too much help upsets the joy and magic of play. Some people believe there is no such child as a stupid child – there is only a stupid parent who makes play too difficult. Not enough help can mean lack of learning, and the loss of pleasure which comes from showing-off a newly-learned skill. When a new skill is learned, praise and encouragement are better than sweets. Sweets are rewards or prizes outside the child. They dull the true reward of all learning – the child's own inner satisfaction at his achievement.

Toys

From an early age, a baby needs the right kind of toys to play with. They do not have to cost money: wooden spoons, plastic drinking cups, bowls of water, make perfect learning toys. He does not need too many; this will only confuse him.

Very different toys are not always as much fun as they seem. The child's small world needs small new additions, not sudden great changes. A difficult construction kit instead of his box of old bricks may bring on tears in an eighteen-month-old.

Safety, and other points to consider

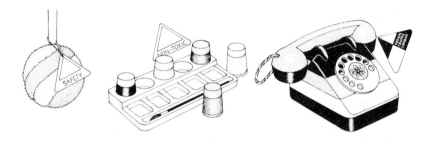

1   As babies feel with their mouths, toys must be too big to swallow or choke on.
2   They must be unbreakable, and free from lead paint which is poisonous.
3   They must be easy to clean, as the baby does not have much resistance to germs until he is at the crawling stage.
4   Soft toys must have passed the safety standard. Eyes stuck in on pins and limbs attached by hooks have caused terrible accidents in the past.
5   For older children, toys need to be sturdy and built to last.
6   There must be no sharp edges, no pins or staples, to cause damage.
7   Toys on wheels should be stable, wheels and brakes regularly checked.
8   Water and sand play need to be supervised. A child should never be left alone playing in the bath or the kitchen sink.
9   Plastic bags must be removed from toys and immediately put away. Most bags carry warnings of the danger of suffocation.
10 To avoid bitter disappointment, check there are batteries to fit any battery-operated toys.

Questions

1   **Why is play important for all children?**
2   **What is meant by 'play progresses in a definite time sequence'? Explain in your own words, giving one example.**
3   **Explain why a child who is ill stops learning.**
4   **Give one example of how a parent helps a child move forward in his play.**
5   **In what way can too much help be wrong?**
6   **Why are sweets not the true reward for learning? Explain as simply as you can.**
7   **Write out five safety points to consider when buying a toy.**
8   **Why should a child never be left playing alone in a paddling-pool?**

Suggestions for toys

At three months

Bright shiny rings and rattles with interesting shapes.
Coloured ribbon or streamers, mobiles, swinging above cot or pram.

From six to nine months

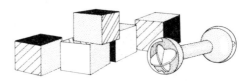

Jangly bells, wooden bricks, plastic spoons for learning hand skills.
Teething ring with small rattle inside for biting and shaking.
Saucepan and lid for banging: blocks for knocking down.

By the first birthday

Fluffy toy: not too large: can be hand-made or bought.
Baby walker, sturdy box on wheels for improving walking skills.
Bath toys: plastic duck, cups, any floating container which is safe.
Blocks, bricks, cotton reels, empty cartons, spinning top, ball.

At two

Large brightly painted and decorated strong cardboard box with child's name
in big letters. Converts to house when empty; toys kept tidily in it at night.
Picture book with large simple drawings – can be hand-made.
Fat wax crayons and drawing paper – unused wall-paper or paper bags will do.
Teddy, rag doll, any stuffed animal for cuddling and lugging around.
Peg-boards, rings on sticks, small dust-pan and brush.

At three

Picture books with simple story to go with the large drawings.
Powder-paints, big brushes, home-made easel. Blackboard and chalks.
Clay, plasticene, dough, sand; bucket and spade, plastic shape-cutters.
Model farm, Noah's ark, toy shop; kitchen, cooking, tea-party equipment.
Tricycle, rocking-horse, wheelbarrow, pram, home-made go-kart or truck.
Old scarves, ties, shoes, junk jewellery without pins for dressing-up.

At four

Paste, blunt-ended scissors, postcards, old magazines, for scrapbook.
Jigsaws, bead-threading kits, simple construction kits.
Planks, boxes, barrels, balls, see-saw, slide, climbing frame, swing.
A selection of story books, some with nursery rhymes and riddles.
A special dressing-up box: old shirts, skirts, scraps from jumble sales.
Toy tool kit, watering can, ironing board, sewing kit, drum, xylophone.

Between five and seven

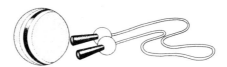

Dominoes, ludo, snakes and ladders, card games for 'snap', 'happy families'.
Abacus, wooden clock, books with alphabet letters and numbers.
Modelling kits; simple pieces to be glued together and painted.
Skipping rope, scooter, small bicycle, football, small ball joined to bat.
Sketch pad, fully equipped pencil case and paint box.
Gardening tools, simple carpentry sets, knitting and embroidery kits.

Questions

1 **Name two toys for a one-year-old which can be found in any home.**
2 **Name three toys for a two-year-old which can be made by parents.**
3 **Name three toys for a three-year-old which you would prefer to buy from a shop.**
4 **Name four toys for a school child which help him with his lessons.**
5 **What toys would you choose to help a child with make-believe play?**
6 **Name three toys which help a child develop outdoor body skills.**
7 **Pick and make a list of all the toys which you think help a child with his intellectual development.**

Books

Books help a child's mental development in a variety of ways. They light up his imagination, stimulate his curiosity, widen his horizons, reinforce his memory, mirror his life, comfort his fears . . . A child who is read to develops a delight in books, and a desire to learn to read for himself.

First books

They must have simple, large, brightly-coloured pictures. A nine-month-old enjoys sitting on parent's knee and staring at the interesting patterns and shapes. At eighteen months, he recognizes familiar pictures. He points, staring up at his parent, waiting for the word he knows but cannot yet say. At two, he turns the pages, delighted to be able to call out the names.

Picture books with stories

Children can read by seven; some read earlier, a few much later. It takes a long time to 'crack the code' of squiggly shapes (letters), and to work out that when they are placed in different sequences, they form different words. Until the child reaches this stage, he should be able to 'read' the plot of the story from what is being shown in the pictures. This is why the best children's books are illustrated with a great deal of care. It is enormously satisfying for the child to be able to see what is going on, while listening to the words being read by parents.

1 *Repetition and rhythm*
'I'll huff and I'll puff and I'll blow your house down.' Repetition helps the child conserve (memorize) the words. A well-constructed sentence has a flowing rhythm too. The child chants aloud in rhythm with the parent; sharing his pleasure, making the story his own.

2 *Tales of adventure*
These widen the child's experience of life. 'The owl and the pussy-cat went to sea in a beautiful pea-green boat.' The more fantastic the story, the greater its

appeal. In the child's fantasy world, anything can change into anything. He is likely to imagine himself sitting in the boat too.

3 *Tales of terror*
'"You must be fattened up for cooking," the witch cackled at Hansel and Gretel.' Witches, wolves or giants gobbling up little children seem terrifying to parents, and most unsuitable as stories. But many children beg to hear them; they act as a release for their own inner tensions and fears. However, parents need to take care with very young or very sensitive children. They must check to make sure the story always has an equally powerful happy ending.

4 *Tales of reassurance*
'At the doctor's, Zoe said "Ouch", but she stood quite still.' These tales are very useful after the child has been through an upset. They mirror the experience: the child is able to relive his bad feelings, and be reassured. However, if the upset was very painful or is yet to happen – going to hospital – the story is more often told as happening to an animal instead of a child.

5 *Tales of everyday*
Children love stories about themselves, ordinary events which have happened during the day. 'Zoe did the washing-up. She turned on the taps . . .' The child listens with intense concentration, correcting the parent when a detail is missed out. Tales of everyday help the child see himself more clearly; slowly he begins to build up an image of who he is.

Suggestions for books

Up to three
The very hungry caterpillar E. Carle, Puffin Books 1974
One fish, two fish Dr Seuss, Collins 1962
Picture stories R. Peppe, Kestrel 1976
Cat on the mat/The trunk B. Wildsmith, OUP 1981
Ladybird picture books

Over three
The mother goose treasury R. Briggs, Puffin 1976
Longman picture dictionary, 1982
Number of things H. Oxenbury, Heinemann 1976
ABC J. Burningham, Jonathan Cape 1974
Little me books D. Manley, Longman 1980
The three little pigs B. Root & D. Oliver, Macdonald Educational 1976
Lucy and Tom go to school S. Hughes, Gollancz 1973
Pelican B. Wildsmith, OUP 1982

Questions

1 **Name four ways in which books help a child's mental development.**
2 **At what age would you begin to show a picture book to a child?**
3 **In your own words, explain the importance of illustrations in books.**
4 **In what ways do stories full of repetition and rhyme help a child?**
5 **What precautions must parents take before reading a tale of terror?**

Milestones of mental development

1   The two-year-old likes scribbling with crayons: jagged lines, round scribbles and dots. He can build a tower of six bricks or plastic cubes. He recognizes and names familiar objects in picture books: 'man', 'ball', 'dolly'. Echolalia (lalia means tongue) is frequent: repeating the sounds of new words over and over again. He joins in nursery rhymes and songs, and talks to himself nonstop while he plays. He can use at least fifty words, and understands many more.

2   The three-year-old draws parent's face; likes to paint with a large brush. He can build a tower of nine blocks and make a bridge of three. He has a large vocabulary, and can take part in simple conversations. He still talks to himself, chatting about what he is doing at play. He knows several nursery rhymes, and demands to hear his favourite stories over and over again. He asks so many questions he is rather like a walking question mark.

Helping with mental development

By three, a child is usually ready for nursery school or playgroup. He needs help to make sense of his world. Perceptions can be puzzling things: they do not always make sense. 'The moon comed up from the top of the house' – which it appeared to – and the child forms the misconception of the moon living in the house. He has to turn puzzling perception into logical thought, and he needs information to do this. It will take him many years at school before he can; but he is starting on the road to cognitive thinking.

Nursery schools, nursery classes, and playgroups

These schools and groups:
(a)   provide children with the company they need.
(b)   provide children with practical experience of play directed towards an understanding of basic concepts.

1   Over a two-year period, the child is encouraged to recognize and name:
(a)   four primary colours, and at least three secondary ones.
(b)   squares, triangles, circles, and rectangles.
(c)   all familiar objects in the building, and at home.
(d)   numbers, by counting games and number rhymes.
(e)   a few letters of the alphabet.

2   His vocabulary is expanded to help him form such concepts as:
(a)   over/under, higher/lower, before/behind.
(b)   thick/thin, short/tall, wide/narrow, full/empty, light/dark.
(c)   too many/too few, bigger than/smaller than, lighter than/heavier than.

3   He learns to match things, working out samenesses and differences.
He learns the functions of things, what they can or cannot be used for.
He learns the properties of things; weight, volume, space, time, length.

Learning co-operative play.

4 He learns co-operative play: to construct, to share, to take turns with other children of his own age. He learns about the rules of games, especially outdoor activities such as ball games.

Learning at home

There may be no suitable playgroup near parents, and not all children are ready at three for the company of more than one other child. Parents can supply all these forms of learning at home. The equipment does not have to be expensive. For example, kitchen scales and measuring jugs are perfect for weighing and volume games. Brothers and sisters will make up the company. An only child should have a playmate. Parents can ask at the clinic or put an advertisement in the local shop window.

Questions

1 **What is meant by 'echolalia', and at what age is it frequent?**
2 **Name the differences between a child's ability to draw and build towers at two and at three.**
3 **Name four things a child is encouraged to recognize and name at nursery class.**
4 **What is meant by 'co-operative' play?**
5 **In your own words, explain how a child can learn at home just as well.**

Habituation (memory patterns)

During the first years of life and the very fast growth of the brain, the memory starts to set down certain patterns, e.g. how to run. A footballer does not have to think before he lifts one foot off the ground, nor about moving his weight from one leg to the other. If he had to stop and work out such simple things each time he moved, he would not be much use at scoring a goal. He knows how to run without thinking (without paying attention). His memory has set down a pattern for running so his mind is free to concentrate on aiming the ball straight into the net. This 'freeing of the mind' to get on with more important things is called habituation (which comes from the word 'habit').

Learning how to run

A small child must 'pay attention' to these simple actions. He is learning them for the first time, and they are very difficult. He needs to practise and practise before he can run without thinking. He falls down many times before the memory gets the pattern right. Think of the cuts and scabs on a seven- or eight-year-old's knees!

This one-year-old girl is just starting to learn to walk. The pattern is not yet set in her memory.

The importance of positive (helpful) teaching

Once a pattern is set down, it is likely to stay in the memory for ever. So it is important the child learns the correct patterns quite early. If, at three, the child still gets his feet tangled, for example, his parents help him 'pay attention' to running in a gentle and encouraging way. It is nasty to fall over again and again; the bumps really hurt. Without help and encouragement, he might decide running is too dangerous. If parents do not teach the child, the physical education teacher at school will help. This takes a long time as the memory of wrong running has to be 'unlearned' before the correct way can be learned.

What happens if teaching is negative (unhelpful)?

At four, Tim still runs sideways, like a crab. He keeps bumping into things. His parents scold him: 'Clumsy, don't run in that silly way.' He is not clumsy; he is making mistakes as all learners do. He hates being told off; his movements get jerkier and more awkward. He is 'paying attention' to his upset feelings instead of learning how to run properly. Negative teaching spoils most things the child needs to learn. A child sees himself as parents see him. If he is told he is clumsy, then he will become clumsy. If he is told he is improving, then his movements will improve. Positive teaching reinforces his good ideas about himself. Negative teaching reinforces his bad ideas.

Summary

1 The memory sets down certain patterns in the early years (habituation).
2 They are useful because they free the mind to concentrate on learning other things.
3 They cannot be laid down until an action has been thoroughly learned.
4 Once this happens, the patterns usually stay for the rest of life.
5 It is very important indeed that the memory stores the right kind of patterns.
6 It is nearly always extremely difficult to unlearn early habituation.

Questions

1   *Charles is told he is a messy eater. His mother still spoon-feeds him at five. During lunch-time at school, the children jeer and call him names. He turns white and is sick all down his new uniform.*
Write down what you think has gone wrong with Charles' learning. What would you think his mother should do to make things better?
2   *Mary's mother works on night-shift and Dad gets the children ready for school. He bundles them into their clothes and puts on their shoes. The teacher tells the class to change their outdoor shoes and hang up their coats and scarves. Mary cannot do these things. She hides in the lavatory and weeps.*
What can the teacher do to make things better for Mary?
3   **What is meant by 'positive' teaching? Why is it important?**
4   **Copy out and learn all the points in the summary.**
5   **'Parents are the child's most important teachers.' Explain why this is true from what you have learned about memory patterns.**

Language (1)

Crying

A baby is born with powerful needs: he cries for what he must be given. Until he learns language, he communicates his needs by crying. He cries for food, warmth, company. He cries from pain and upset feelings. If he did not cry, parents could not know when something was wrong. Crying is an essential part of a baby's survival kit. Crying stops when a baby is picked up and given what he needs.

How children learn language

A three-year-old does not suddenly know how to talk. He had been learning about language non-stop from the day he was born. He learns by listening to words, and by practising sounds (vocalizing).

At three months, he gurgles, grunts, coos, when he is spoken to, or alone.

At six months, he turns immediately to the sound of his mother's voice and croons happily at her.

By nine months, he babbles tunefully; shouts for attention instead of crying; understands 'no-no'; says 'maamm-mam, da-dad, bab-bab'.

By one year, he babbles almost non-stop. He turns immediately on hearing his name. Understands 'clap hands, give to Daddy, pick up spoon'.

By two, he uses 50+ words; understands many more. He talks aloud to his toys when playing, echoes parents' words, and points correctly to parts of his face.

By three, he uses 200+ words. He talks in short sentences, asks questions 'who, what, why', talks non-stop to toys in make-believe play.

By five, his speech is fluent. Words in sentences are in correct grammatical order. He knows favourite stories by heart, and sings and chants nursery rhymes.

By seven, he has learned almost fifty per cent of the vocabulary of an eighteen-year-old. Many children are reading and writing quite well by this time.

Feeding the mind with words

Deaf babies go through the stages of cooing and babbling. But they do not go on to speak words, without very special help. They cannot learn language because they do not hear words spoken.

Language is a basic human need. It makes shape and sense of thought. Babies and small children must be spoken to as much as possible. The best time for learning the most language is long before school.

Not too little

Some babies are not spoken to because parents think it unnecessary. They do not understand it is important to speak directly to the baby. By two, the child naturally tries to copy his parents' conversation. It is too difficult. He fails; parents laugh; he stops trying. He has no picture books to point at objects and

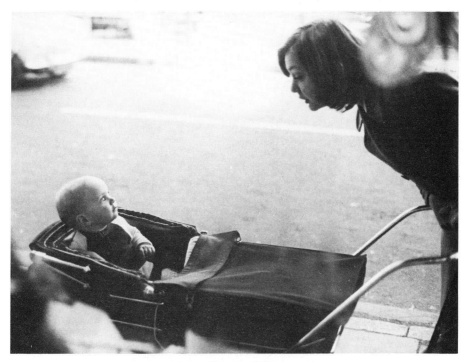

A baby learns by listening to words, and by practising sounds.

name them, no crayons or drawing-paper, no bed-time story, no rhymes or nursery chants. When he arrives at school and cannot understand the language, he (a) pretends not to care and causes a nuisance, or (b) is too timid and unhappy to settle down to learn.

Not too much

Some parents are over-keen to have a clever child. They keep correcting his pronunciation. They are cross when he uses the wrong words. If he asks a simple question, he gets a far too complicated answer. He is forced to practice letters, forced to listen to difficult stories. He is bullied and nagged; he turns fretful and stubborn. The joy and pleasure of language are killed before he starts school.

Questions

1 **At what age does a child first start learning about language?**
2 **What will a six-month-old do when he hears his mother's voice?**
3 **Write down two things a one-year-old can usually say.**
4 **How many words does the average child know at two?**
5 **Why do deaf babies not learn to speak without very special help?**
6 **Why should parents speak to their under-fives as much as possible?**
7 **Why is language so important? Give at least two reasons for your answer.**
8 **Write a short essay about the dangers of (a) over- and (b) under-stimulation of language.**

Language (2)

The right kind of language

Baby coos, mother smiles 'what a clever noise'. She coos back. She talks to him directly, smiling into his eyes (eye contact). She asks 'are you hungry? does the bath water feel good?' long before he can answer. She is teaching him the way people communicate.

When she says 'Mummy is making soup for dinner', she explains what she is doing, and gives him information about her work. She repeats the words, altering them slightly: 'this is baby's dinner Mummy is getting ready', and he learns different ways of saying things. His first real words are greeted with pride and joy. He squeals with delight, and tries again. He loves pleasing his parents.

Father points to different objects in the picture book.
The child 'watches with mother' to have the difficult bits explained.

Dad chants nursery rhymes, plays naming games, points to different objects in his picture book. The child tries hard to remember the new words. When he asks questions, he gets clear simple answers that he understands. Television programmes for the pre-school child are usually very good. He 'watches with mother' to have the difficult bits explained. The television is switched off at the end of the programme so he can act out what he has seen; practising the songs and stories till he knows them. Dad invents or reads the bed-time story. He watches the child to make sure the tale is neither too difficult, nor too frightening. Neither parent forces the child to learn. They stop at once if he begins to look bored, or tired. Word-games must always be fun. Parents reward their child's new language with praise, hugs, kisses. They correct only a few mistakes, and with hugs so he does not feel he has failed.

Between the ages of three and four, words may spill out so quickly there may be some stammering. Parents calm an excitable child and ignore the stammering. It is natural at this stage for a child to stammer, or lisp, or suddenly go back to baby talk. There are so many exciting things he wants to say! If the parents get anxious and try to correct this natural stage, the child may grow anxious too. He may begin to stutter. Speech disorders later on can sometimes be traced back to a child's unhappy feelings at this stage. If the stammer gets worse by the time the child is five, parents (a) check the child is not anxious about anything else at home; (b) ask at the clinic or school for hearing tests; (c) make an appointment with the speech therapist who will give advice and may suggest speech therapy lessons.

Language at home

1 The importance of language at home cannot be stressed strongly enough.
2 Parents can try to keep their words as rich and varied as possible.
3 Children do not learn many words from other children of their own age.
4 It is grown-ups who know the strange new interesting language.
5 Constant noise from radio, television, cassette, record-player, will limit or stop family conversation altogether.
6 Mealtimes with family chats, gossip, and jokes are ideal for the child to hear new words, and take part in the conversation.

Questions

1 **Name three things a baby learns when his mother talks to him before he can understand what she says.**
2 **Write down three things a father can do to help his child learn language.**
3 **Why does a pre-school child need company when watching television?**
4 **Why should the set be switched off at the end of the programme?**
5 **Explain in your own words what advice you would give to a parent who is worried about a three-year-old beginning to stammer.**
6 **What three things can parents do if the child is not speakingly fluently by five?**
7 **Explain why a four-year-old cannot learn many new words from another four-year-old.**

Language (3)

*'I keep six honest serving men
(They taught me all I knew);
Their names are What and Why and When
And How and Where and Who.'*

(Rudyard Kipling)

Asking questions

To learn about the grown-up world, a child must ask questions: 'Why do the postman whistle?' – answer – 'Why is he happy?' – answer -- 'What do happy mean?' – answer – 'Do you buy happy in letters?' – answer -- 'Is trees happy?' (Silent groans – 'Will he ever stop asking questions?')

Parents can actually groan aloud when they hear yet another question! But the small child is curious: he wants reasons for everything. He thinks his parents know all the answers, and are only too delighted to give him the information he needs.

Instead of saying 'Oh, do shut up!', the child can be asked to draw a happy tree, a happy postman – or whatever his questions are about. Besides giving the parent a break, this gives the child time to sort out ideas about whistling, and being happy: how people show happiness but objects do not, and so on.

Bizarre questions

*'Why did that man be a snake?'
'Where do time fly past to go?'
'How do that lady make big for her boots?'*

Bizarre questions come from confusions about grown-ups' conversations. He cannot understand what he hears: the words do not make sense. He asks questions because he knows language explains the world; gives shape and meaning to his thoughts. He is too little to understand concepts: he takes speech literally. Story books need pictures to avoid this kind of confusion, too.

'Once upon a time, a bat saw some hares at the fork of the road.'

Limited powers of reasoning

Two equal-sized beakers were filled with equal amounts of (a) milk, (b) water. Children between five and seven were asked 'is milk bigger than water?' Though beakers and the amounts of liquid were identical, their answers went something like this:

Yes, because milk tastes more.
Yes, because there's white in it.
Yes, because it makes teeth grow.
Yes, because you buy it from the milkman.
Yes, because you don't have your bath in it.

Mixed messages

'Doesn't he look charming with that yucky runny nose!'
'Oh yes, Dad's very proud when his little girl spits out her dinner!'

Children learn from the parents' <u>tone</u> that they really mean the opposite of their words. But sarcasm is particularly difficult to understand when they begin to learn language. The child (a) listens to the words, (b) works out their meaning, (c) flinches away from the nasty tone, (d) is bewildered, muddled, shocked, upset.

Only a poor-quality teacher in junior school uses sarcasm on children. It is negative teaching as far as language development is concerned. Parents of pre-school children need to understand that sarcastic jokes may well amuse adults, but should be kept from children while they struggle to make sense of their world.

Questions

1 **Why does Rudyard Kipling call questions 'honest serving men'?**
2 **From what you have learned about 'paying attention', why do you think you are asked so many questions in this book?**
3 **Why does a small child ask questions all the time? Give at least two reasons for your answer.**
4 **Give one example to show the way in which a child 'takes speech literally'.**
5 **In your own words, explain why it is best to avoid sarcastic remarks when speaking to a small child.**

Further work on Chapter 5

1 Watch the work of an experienced play-leader. Write down what you observe of the ways she helps the children move forward in play.

2 Observe outdoor play. Make notes on which kind of swings are most popular with children of different ages.

3 Visit a toy shop. Do a full project on toys for a child of any age under seven, with detailed notes on cost, safety, durability, interest, and learning potential.

4 Make a toy for a child under seven. Write down the reasons why you chose that particular toy and give details of how you made it.

5 Visit the children's section in the local library. Do a project on books suitable for (a) a two-year-old and (b) a five-year-old. If necessary, ask the librarian for help and advice. Find out and write about toy libraries.

6 Make a scrap book to entertain a lively four-year-old. Use cut-outs from magazines, nursery rhymes, jokes, number games.

7 Collect pictures drawn by children of three, five, seven. Make notes on what you observe of a child's growing understanding of his world.

8 'Toys for children are so expensive nowadays.' Write a short essay, explaining why this statement does not have to be true.

9 Try to get as much practical experience of playing with children as you can. Offer to assist, but bear in mind that your strangeness may frighten a small child. Keep detailed notes of (a) the ways you approached the child, (b) the way the child reacted, (c) the games you played together, (d) what you learned from the experience.

10 Read a story to a child under seven. Make notes of his reactions – did he repeat certain words, point at the pictures, ask questions, and so on?

11 In early childhood, play is one of the principal ways of learning. Explain this statement by giving examples of how play activities help to develop:
   (a) language
   (b) physical skills
   (c) social behaviour
   (d) intellect
   (e) imagination. (EAEB)

12 Discuss how adults may assist the intellectual development of children from birth to five years of age. (SUJB)

13 Language encourages intellectual development.
   (a) State four reasons why a child needs to communicate by using language.
   (b) Describe three stages in the development of language and explain how the adult can help at each stage.
   (c) Suggest how three different activities at playgroup could encourage language development.
   (d) Describe with examples three ways language helps intellectual development.
   (e) In what ways does a good vocabulary help a child to be independent when he starts school? (SWEB)

Chapter 6

Emotional health: development of the feelings

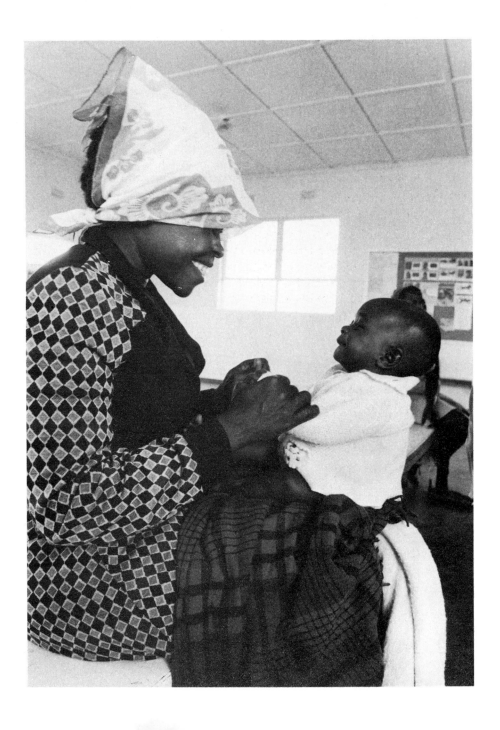

About the emotions

Love	Hate
Joy	Sorrow
Daring	Fear
Desire	Aversion
Hope	Despair

This list of the emotions was written many centuries ago. There are more modern lists: some longer, some shorter. The emotions people have do not change, whatever list is chosen. The above emotions are common to all people, in all places, in all times.

Positive and negative

The list on the left are the good – the positive emotions. The list on the right seem to be the bad ones – the negative emotions. For each positive emotion, there is an opposite negative one. It seems that human emotions are fairly evenly balanced up.

A better world?

Would life be wonderful if people felt only the positive emotions? Why do people have negative emotions if they are the bad ones? Could negative emotions be wiped out if we lived in a better world?

Points to consider:

It is natural for a child to hate being 'told off', to feel great sorrow when his beloved pet dies, to fear fast-moving traffic, and so on. What might happen to a six-year-old who did not fear traffic? What about a twenty-year-old? How could there be acts of great daring if there was no great fear?

Mixed emotions.

People are fascinating because they have such very complicated emotions. They will weep with joy and sorrow at their favourite piece of music! They can feel hate towards the very person they most love! It seems the negative emotions will exist long after we have made a better world. It seems we cannot think of the negative emotions as bad, except in certain special circumstances.

Special circumstances

People have conflicts of emotions – their feelings are at war. This is natural. No-one can fulfil all their hopes, all the time. During times of unhappiness, people try to keep some balance in their feelings: 'If Winter comes, can Spring be far behind?' (*Shelley*). The negative emotions are bad when this kind of balance is lost. The unhappy feelings go on so long that the person becomes ill.

The child's psychological make-up

It is important to understand how a child can be helped to keep a healthy balance between the positive and negative emotions. The affective (p. 107) sides of his nature must be cared for as well as the cognitive (p. 107) sides. For the purpose of study, mental and emotional development are discussed here in two separate chapters, but it is, in fact, very difficult to separate them. The personality of the child, his psychological make-up, is a combination of the working of the mind and emotions together.

Questions

1 **Copy out the list of emotions. Are there other emotions you think should be added, or some which should be removed?**
2 **If you lived in Timbuktu, do you think your emotions would be any different from those you have where you live now?**
3 **Look up the meaning of the word 'aversion'. Write two different sentences which show you understand the meaning clearly.**
4 **Is it natural for a child to have negative emotions? Can you think of two other examples where it is natural?**
5 **Give one example of how people feel opposite emotions at the same time.**
6 **In your own words, explain why the negative emotions can be called 'bad' in certain circumstances.**

About the balance of the emotions

Student Zoe fails her exams. They were very important. She is filled with hate and despair. 'It is the end of my life,' Zoe weeps. She feels very unhappy for a long long time. But even as she weeps, she knows it is not the end of her life. She plans other things she could do: she wonders if she should re-sit the exam. Zoe is coping with stress.

Student Zack fails his important exams. He is filled with exactly the same emotions as Zoe. 'It is the end of my life,' Zack insists. He is sure the teachers and examiners plotted against him. He plans to punish the world: suicide will teach the world a lesson or two. In the end, he does not kill himself, but he does become mentally ill.

Balance

Why do Zoe and Zack have such different ways of reacting to stress? At the beginning, both students' reactions were perfectly normal. Why did Zack not recover from being knocked off balance?

Everyone has stress in their lives at one time or another. But people know that, given time, damaged emotions do mend: they do get better.

Mental health

1　Zoe is well-balanced emotionally.
2　Though she weeps, she secretly knows it is not the end of her life.
3　She knows her emotions will get better. She is mentally healthy.

Mental ill-health

1　Zack is unbalanced emotionally.
2　He insists on believing that failing exams is the end of the world.
3　He cannot believe his emotions will mend. He is mentally ill.

Nature or nurture?

Babies have stress, and so do small children. Some of the ways people cope with stress later in life depends on what happened when they suffered stress as children. Did something go wrong for Zack when he was a baby? Or was he born with very fragile emotions? Who can say?

It is important to remember we do not know what people inherit. But some parents do say their baby was born placid. Other parents say their baby was born excitable. It seems likely babies inherit a 'tendency' to be placid or excitable; though it is difficult to classify human temperament – many babies are somewhere in between.

Points to consider

1. A baby's first emotional experiences are always with adults. This seems obvious enough, but it is sometimes forgotten.
2. The happy 'placid' baby smiles sweetly, cooing his delight at parents.
3. The happy 'excitable' baby yells joyfully, wriggling with pleasure.
4. But when either baby is unhappy, they behave to parents in much the same way; they whimper, cry, then scream loudly.
5. These very angry noises happen because the baby needs things put right: he needs to feel good.
6. Babies have an inborn drive to experience the positive emotions, i.e. to be happy, no matter what their temperament.

Laughter is infectious.

In the early years of life, adults are the people with whom children share their emotions.

Questions

1. **Copy out the three points on 'mental health' and 'mental ill-health'.**
2. **What do you think being 'emotionally well-balanced' means?**
3. **Do all babies, whatever their temperament, need to be happy?**
4. **Who are the people a baby shares his early positive and negative emotions with?**

Mother-love

Mother-love can be given to a baby by any caring adult.

'Mother-love in infancy and childhood is as important for mental health as are vitamins and proteins for physical health.'

What does mother-love mean?

Dr John Bowlby, a famous child psychiatrist, wrote the words above in 1951. The study of the growth of children's emotions is fairly recent. Now, a lot of people have a lot of different ideas about what love means. Some call it warmth, or affection, or bonding. A few tough-minded people think it all rather soppy. They insist all a baby needs is to be fed, and kept warm and clean.

The argument

No one argues about vitamins and proteins being important for physical growth and health. A child who lacks these foods in his diet will not develop well. Everyone can <u>see</u> this, so there is no reason to argue. However, many people still argue about the importance of mother-love. The results <u>cannot be seen</u> so clearly: the growth of healthy emotions is not an easy thing to measure, like height.

Studies on mother-love

It has been found there is a link between mother-love and healthy physical development of the child. In old-style nurseries and children's homes (orphanages), there were not enough nurses to spend time playing with and 'loving-up' the children. When their development was measured against children's from loving homes, it was found they were backward in walking, talking and so on.

The evidence of poor emotional development

In these children's homes, some of the babies and small children lay quiet and still. They did not smile. They did not play. They looked sad and frightened. Others were very noisy and cried a great deal. They banged their heads very hard on the cot rails, as if trying to bang away their misery. Still others begged for attention from any person who was near. They could not tell the difference between strangers and nurses.

Mother-love

Mother-love can be given to a baby by any caring adult. Dr Bowlby called it 'mother-love' because the adult is usually the mother. But father, aunt, grandparents, adopting or fostering parents can all fulfil the baby's need for mother-love just as well. Just as long as:

1 The child is valued for his own sake; for the person he or she is.
2 The child is valued whether boy or girl; attractive or plain; placid or excitable.
3 The child is valued no matter what his personality, or his talents.
4 The child is valued without any conditions: e.g. that he sleeps through the night, smiles cutely, eats up his dinner, and so on.
5 Mother-love is unconditional love. It is one of the highest forms of human loving.

Bonding

The flow of unconditional love from mother to baby is called bonding. The mother adores the baby 'warts and all' quite soon after birth. Sadly, in a few mothers, bonding does not happen 'naturally' or easily. In some cases, the mothers themselves did not get love when they were babies.

The first days after birth are vital for bonding, so babies are now put in mothers' arms instead of being whisked off to the nursery. Mothers who fear they will not be able to love their babies must not think they are 'unnatural'. They need help and advice before the baby is born; at the antenatal clinic or from the family doctor.

Questions

1 **Copy out and learn the quote from Dr John Bowlby.**
2 **Copy out 'The evidence of poor emotional development'.**
3 **Who else can give a baby unconditional love, apart from his mother?**
4 **In your own words, say what unconditional love means.**
5 **What is the most important time for mothers to bond with their babies?**
6 **What should a mother do if she is afraid she will not love her baby?**

The importance of unconditional love

The first months

The baby is helpless; he cannot fetch food, stay warm, keep dry. He depends absolutely on his parents for these things. He needs parents to take care of him when he is unhappy; when he is cold, thirsty, hungry, lonely, unwell. He cries to warn his parents that things do not feel right.

A parent who loves unconditionally:

1 Goes to the baby as soon as he calls.
2 Makes sure he stops feeling hungry or thirsty.
3 Makes sure he feels clean and warm and dry.
4 Talks and plays with him so he begins to learn about life.
5 Picks him up and cuddles him so he feels wanted and loved.

What the baby shows of his feelings

At first, the baby has no idea his parents are marvellous. During feeding, he stares straight into his mother's eyes. This is called 'eye-to-eye contact'; he seems to study her closely.

By three months, he shows happy excitement when she plays with him. He stops crying because he 'knows' she will put things right. By six months, he is strongly attached to her. She brings him happiness. By nine months, he beams at his family, but is frightened of strangers. By the age of three, he seems confident, happy and eager for life.

The results of unconditional love

It must be very frightening to be absolutely helpless. It is only natural to cry out in terror at feeling so unsafe. It must be marvellous when hunger or cold pains are taken away. No wonder a baby spends so long gazing at his parents' faces. During the first years, he learns he can trust his parents. Whenever he cries out, they come and make him feel better. He knows he is safe: he feels he belongs in a secure happy place. He feels 'good' in himself, 'good' about his parents, 'good' about the world he is in.

Later on

The 'good' feelings the child develops are the positive emotions. His self-image (how he thinks of himself) is positive: stable and secure. A person with a positive self-image is free to develop the other sides of his personality. He is confident and eager to learn. When things go wrong, he does not have to stop and 'pay attention' to his damaged feelings for too long. He gets on with life while his feelings mend: they always got better quickly when he was a baby and his parents were there to help. The memory patterns of how people feel are – like learning how to run – laid down in early childhood. Unconditional love during the first years of life helps the growth of positive emotions in much the same way as vitamin D and calcium helps the growth of strong teeth and bones.

Questions

1 **Name four reasons why a baby cries.**
2 **Copy out the things a parent who loves unconditionally will do.**
3 **Why do you think babies sometimes feel very frightened?**
4 **During the first years, what are the results of unconditional love on the small child's feelings?**
5 **Explain in your own words what is meant by a 'positive self-image'.**
6 **When are the memory patterns of people's self-images first laid down?**

Conditional love

A parent who loves in a grudging sort of way:

1   Lets the baby cry, hoping he will exhaust himself back to sleep.
2   Makes the baby wait, till the parent decides he is hungry or thirsty.
3   Does not change a cold wet nappy, the baby will only wet a clean one.
4   Hurries through bath and feed time, upset because it takes so long.
5   Thinks picking up and cuddles are wrong, they only spoil the baby.

What the baby shows of his feelings

At first, the baby has no idea parents are less than marvellous. During feeding he stares straight up into his mother's eyes. He misses eye-to-eye contact, but he studies her closely.

By three months, he shows great excitement when she comes for the next feed. In between, he cries a lot because he 'knows' things are not put right. By six months, he is attached to her. She brings him food, which is good. By nine months, he cries fretfully for the attention he is not getting. By the age of three, he appears whining and demanding; clinging and insecure.

The results of conditional love

Being left to cry when things are wrong makes a baby feel much worse. When he is picked up, he cannot be easily calmed and soothed. He is in great panic; tense and over-exhausted with fear. Parents think he is 'difficult': he is playing up on purpose. During the first years the baby learns he cannot trust parents much. It seems his feelings do not matter when nobody bothers to put them right. But they do matter. He feels they matter. His world seems very unsafe. He feels 'bad' about himself, 'bad' about his parents, 'bad' about the world he is in.

Later on

The 'bad' feelings the child develops are the negative emotions. His self-image is low. He feels negative, confused, insecure, angry. A person with a negative self-image is not free to develop other sides of his personality. He may want to learn, but he lacks confidence. When things go wrong, he cannot 'pay attention' to putting them right, or trying something different. The memory patterns of his feelings start up the same panics he felt when he was tiny and under stress. He cannot get on with life while his feelings mend: he does not believe damaged emotions will get better with time. Conditional love during the first years of life helps the growth of negative emotions in much the same way as sweets and sticky foods help the growth of bacteria on the teeth.

Points to consider

1 The emotional patterns of the way people feel about themselves are laid down in early childhood.
2 All habits can be broken. People can stop feeling negative about themselves, but it does take time.
3 Not all people have the same depths (amounts) of feeling. Some are naturally very sensitive, other are not.
4 There are many kinds of mental ill-health which have nothing to do with feelings experienced in early childhood.
5 But as break-downs in adults often can be traced back to early unhappy feelings, parents should know about the results of conditional and unconditional love.
6 A child who feels unloved and insecure will not develop his mind or his body as quickly as a child who feels loved and cherished.
7 Parents and others close to small children need to keep in mind the words of Urie Bronfenbrenner who summarized his research into child development quite simply – 'Somebody has to be crazy about that kid!'

Questions

1 **Copy out the things a parent who loves conditionally will do.**
2 **Explain in your own words why leaving a baby to cry makes things worse.**
3 **During the first years, what are the results of conditional love?**
4 **Explain why a person with a low self-image is not free to develop the rest of his personality.**
5 **Is a person stuck with a negative habit of thinking, or can he change?**
6 **Who is responsible for the emotional health of a small child?**
7 **Write a short essay on the quote 'Somebody has to be crazy about that kid', with references to unconditional love.**

Socialization

A baby reared alone in a cage would have no idea how to behave with other people. He might fight them. He might ignore them. But he would not know what they were for. He would not know how to love, to share, to feel anything for them at all.

What 'socialization' means

'Socialization' means helping a child to fit in with his world. (It is easy to remember because it comes from the word 'social'.) Most parents help their children fit in without thinking. The idea of 'fair shares' is something everyone understands.

The centre of attention

At first, the baby cannot fit in with his family. He is helpless, he cannot look after himself, everything must be done for him. So, for the first years of life, the family fits itself around the baby. Grandparents and siblings help as much as they can. This is one of the ways the family shows unconditional love: putting the baby's needs first, taking shares with the work, baby-minding, and so on. Later on, the small child is no longer the centre of attention. He must take his turn with the rest of the family as that is only fair. If a new baby comes along, he must move one up the ladder.

Fair shares for everyone – except baby

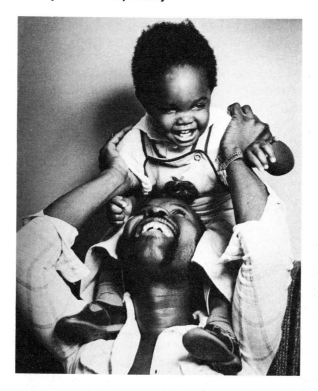

The idea of fair shares is understood by everyone except the small child. He sees parents and toys as part of him, not separate at all. He thinks of the world as being specially there to please or annoy him. He pokes exploring fingers into his father's mouth just to learn what it feels like. He has no idea this may not exactly thrill his father! He dribbles on his mother, bites the edge of the new pram, knocks and bangs at anything which catches his attention. He does what he feels like doing; families put precious objects away and let him get on with it. They know he is exploring, and learning while he is exploring. They know he does not understand – because he is too little to learn – that people have a right not to be poked or dribbled on! And that the things in his home are not there just to please him.

Questions

1 **How might a baby reared alone behave towards other people?**
2 **What does the word 'socialization' mean?**
3 **Why is a new baby not able to fit in with his family?**
4 **Why cannot a small child stay at the centre of attention?**
5 **How does the small baby see his parents, and toys?**
6 **Name three things a baby might do which parents may not find exactly thrilling.**
7 **Do you think it fair that families have to put their precious objects out of the baby's sight? Give reasons for your answer.**
8 **Why do families let a baby get on with his exploring?**

Milestones of emotional learning (1)

It takes a while to learn the difference between 'me' and 'not me'. The baby's parents, especially mother, have to be seen as 'not me' and 'separate from me'. By seven to nine months, the baby knows the difference between family and strangers. He is frightened by unfamiliar faces; he hides his face and cries. This is perfectly normal behaviour and lasts up to the age of three, sometimes longer.

Separation anxiety

1   This is caused by the child's need to be close to his mother and his inner fears that he will lose her.
2   By one year, he screams with anxiety if he is out of sight and hearing of one of his family, usually his mother.
3   By 18 months, he will play alone, but only if mother is somewhere near.
4   At two, he seems ever more dependent on her company, and her reassuring comforting presence.
5   From about six months to three years, a child needs to be close to the few people he knows and loves: mother, father, grandparent, close family friend. If he is separated he shows extreme anxiety and unhappiness.
6   This is perfectly normal behaviour which parents have to expect.

Mothers

Many mothers also get separation anxiety; they cannot bear being too far away from their child either. But there are times when the most loving mother can feel quite frantic at not having any break from her child's constant emotional demands. Some mothers report that they cannot even shut the lavatory door without the child weeping with fear that she has vanished for ever.

In an extended family, a mother does not feel under such constant pressure. The loved and familiar faces of other members of the family stop the child getting anxious when mother is away.

In a nuclear family, father can take the pressure off, but only when he is at home. A mother on her own during the day needs lots of friends who also have small demanding children. Once these friends' faces become familiar and trusted, mothers can take turns at 'group-mothering' while the others have a well-deserved break.

Mother and Toddler Clubs

These clubs may be organized by social workers, health visitors, or the Pre-school Playgroup Association (p. 152); or they may start up quite naturally between a group of mothers. They are of special importance to mothers in high-rise buildings, who can become depressed at the loneliness created by these great impersonal blocks.

Mother and Toddler Clubs offer women a chance to meet and make friends with other mothers. They can discuss the normal worries and difficulties of raising children. They can share their problems as well as sharing their delights. Mothers gain confidence and reassurance from one another's experiences. Situations which may have seemed dreadful at the time (e.g. toddler throwing contents of pot over balcony) become very funny and not at all serious when they are shared. Good company is essential for keeping a balanced outlook on life.

It is likely mothers need and deserve clubs more than any other one group of people. Sportsmen and businessmen and working men are well catered for. A great deal more effort needs to be directed towards the needs of mothers with young children by both government and local policy-makers.

Questions

1 **Between what ages is a child frightened by unfamiliar faces?**
2 **Describe how a child is likely to behave if left alone with a stranger.**
3 **What is meant by 'separation anxiety'? Copy out all the points in the text for your answer.**
4 **Why are Mother and Toddler Clubs specially important for mothers alone in high-rise buildings?**
5 **Name three advantages for women who go to Mother and Toddler Clubs.**
6 **The cost of running a working man's or students' club is usually paid for partly from union funds and partly by personal subscription. Write a short paragraph explaining why this is not possible for many mothers, and the reasons why they need government and local aid to support their clubs.**

Milestones of emotional learning (2)

At home, before two

The child is likely to ignore the family pet, his teddy, the new baby. If he does take notice, he treats them roughly or carelessly. He dumps teddy in the rubbish bin, pulls the cat's tail, throws food at the new baby. Adults may think this is jealousy. It is not. Not yet, anyway. He simply does not understand they are not there to please him. And as a new baby is pretty unexciting, he does not regard it as anything much.

'Mine' and 'not mine'

It is very difficult for a child to learn the meaning of 'mine' and 'not mine'. The food on his sister's plate has to be seen as 'not mine'. And then he has to go on to learn what is 'yours', and what is 'theirs'. Being able to give back a toy means he has learned what is 'yours'. Not stealing sweets from a shop means he has learned what is 'theirs'.

The stage of being egocentric

Thinking the world revolves around you is called being 'egocentric'. This is not the same as having a big ego – being 'egotistical' (big-headed). All small children pass through the stage of being egocentric. It is a nasty shock to learn you are not the centre of the universe! It causes temper tantrums; screaming rages when you are not given what you want immediately and without any arguments! The worst of this stage is usually over by the age of three.

Helping the child safely through

It may be better to sympathize with the child, than to lose patience. Until he knows the difference between 'mine', 'yours', 'theirs', he is totally convinced he has a right to everything which interests him. As most things do interest him, he seems greedy and selfish and bossy. It is important to remember he is not any of these things on purpose. That is the way people are in the beginning. Everyone has to learn to share, to be unselfish, to fit in with others.

A place of his own

It helps if a child has a place of his own to play; under the table will do if there is not much space. He needs an old box in which to keep his carefully-guarded toys. He feels safe because they are his. He learns the pleasures of owning things and looking after them. He begins to understand personal and 'territorial' possession. He begins to learn ideas of the need to respect the rights of other people.

Parallel play

A two-year-old does not play with another child of his own age. He may like the child's company, but he will not play with him. He will play beside him. This is called parallel play. He is not ready to play with other children until about the age of three.

Questions

1 **Name three ways in which an 18-month-old may treat the family pet.**
2 **Explain why the child is not being jealous when he ignores the new baby.**
3 **What does being 'egocentric' mean?**
4 **Would you be angry with a greedy two and a half-year-old, or sympathetic? Give as many reasons as you can for your answer.**
5 **Name three very important things a child begins to learn from having a place of his own, with his own box of toys.**
6 **Copy out and learn what 'parallel play' means.**

Company (1)

By three, a child needs the company of other children. He takes delight in sheer nonsense, and invents wild crazy games from which adults are excluded. A shy child finds it difficult to join in and should not be forced. He gets great pleasure from standing at the edge of a group and watching. At this stage, children study other children with intense concentration and with intense fascination.

The Pre-school Playgroup Association

This is an association run by trained staff who understand the needs of the pre-school child. They are funded by a government grant, but as the amount is so small, playgroups are held in church halls, community centres, or anywhere which is not too expensive. Their play equipment may be very basic – only a few battered home-made toys – or it may be plentiful. This usually depends on the area, and how willing parents are at fund-raising and supplying the group with outgrown or discarded toys. Toy libraries are a useful source of much-needed picture books. Often local businesses donate cash or practical help, for example supplying men to dig the sand-pit, or buying the wood needed for indoor structures.

Mothers are encouraged to stay with their children and to take part in the games and learning. A mother who enjoys cooking may teach the children how to make gingerbread people. Another mother may have sewing skills, teaching the children bead-work and making costumes for dressing up. This kind of community self-help is proving enormously popular. Mothers do not <u>have</u> to stay; they can go off for a break. But many prefer to stay and make friends, enjoying the lively atmosphere and watching their own child learn through play.

Company-sharing

Not all three-year-olds are ready for the hurly-burly of a playgroup. Mothers who have friends can work out a rota system for mornings or afternoons spent in each others' homes. The advantages are much the same as those of the playgroup: lots of company for mothers and children, and the pressure taken off each individual mother.

Baby-sitting

In some homes, parents take turns at baby-sitting. In others, parents refuse to leave their children when they are small. People are different, and what suits one family may make another family very unhappy. Baby-sitting is now so usual, parents needing to get out should not feel guilty. Grandparents and friends make good baby-sitters because the child knows them, but they are not always available.

Requirements for baby-sitting

<u>The child must get to know the baby-sitter.</u> This can be done by hiring the person the day before, and letting her help with tea-time and getting the child ready for bed. Parents can then judge for themselves if the baby-sitter has a warm and sympathetic attitude to children. The baby-sitter has a chance to learn the child's routine, and to understand exactly what is expected of her in meeting the child's needs. Parents must leave a telephone number where they can be contacted in case of emergency. If this is not possible, the baby-sitter should be instructed in simple first aid, and be given the name and address of the family doctor. Once these precautions are taken, parents can enjoy their evening out with no nagging doubts or worries.

Baby-sitters often advertise in local shops. Older teenagers and students can make excellent baby-sitters, especially if they have a genuine interest in children. If parents stay out very late, arrangements should be made either for the baby-sitter to stay overnight or to have a safe means of getting back to her own home.

Questions

1 **At what age is a child ready for the company of other children?**
2 **Name two ways in which mothers can help in their local playgroup.**
3 **Name two sources of supply for materials needed in playgroups.**
4 **Explain the reasons why playgroups are regarded as community self-help groups.**
5 **What is meant by 'company-sharing'?**
6 **Write a short paragraph about baby-sitting, discussing all the points parents need to consider.**

Company (2)

The only child

The only child has many benefits a child from a large family may lack. He may have all his parents' love, time, and energy; he may be talked to more; he may have very expensive toys and clothes and a perfectly-equipped nursery.

Parents of only children have to take care not to over-load with gifts: nor to make a burden of the weight of their love. The only child needs companions of the same age for the mad and silly games between children which parents cannot understand. He misses the jealousy when a new baby is born, and growing through jealousy to love and tenderness – something all siblings have to learn.

Siblings

The child with brothers and sisters may feel he is not getting his fair share of parents' love, time and energy. This is not surprising: the more children in a family, the greater drain on the parents' supply of individual care – and finances. But the advantages of siblings usually far outweigh the disadvantages; though the child may not realize this when he is small.

Learning to be very attached to a close rival is an important lesson in human relationships. Siblings squabble, fight, and bear grudges. But siblings make up, share tender secrets, rush fiercely to one another's defence outside the home. Siblings are not usually lonely: from an early age they begin to learn about sharing and co-operation, about tender and protective feelings. They learn about the limits of aggression (anger attacks) too. Parents quickly stop fights which are too fierce or unequal. Parents understand that sibling rivalry is not surprising. They help the first child over his feelings of jealousy at the new baby by giving him extra love and attention. They make him feel an even more important member of the family now he has moved up one place.

Twins

People sometimes think it would be lovely to have a twin: never to be alone; to have one person who is always very close. But there are disadvantages to being twins, as there are to the only child and to siblings.

Each baby needs a whole relationship with his parents. This is not so easy with twins; a mother cannot respond to their cries equally. Even identical twins are <u>not</u> the same people. They must be treated differently to suit the differences in their temperaments. It is easier to develop a sense of who you are (a clear self-image) if you do not have what seems like a mirror-image nearby all the time.

Twins, left to their own company, do not develop as quickly as other children, especially in language skills. Like all children during the perceptual stage of thinking, they cannot help each other move forward much without adult suggestions, and praise. Because twins have simple communication with each other, their language stays babyish as they do not bother to struggle for words.

Parents help twins develop separate identities and language skills by giving each child separate attention – which can be quite difficult. If someone says 'Hey, you', it is regarded as a bit of an insult. Saying 'Hey, twin', is denying that person the right to his own individual identity.

Questions

1 **Name three advantages and three disadvantages an only child might have.**
2 **In your own words, try to explain how parents could 'make a burden of the weight of their love' to an only child.**
3 **What is meant by sibling rivalry'? Is it natural? Should parents be surprised when their children quarrel?**
4 **What can parents do to help the oldest child get over feelings of jealousy for the new baby?**
5 **Write a short essay on siblings, explaining some of the ways brothers and sisters help one another in their emotional development.**
6 **'Twins are easy to raise because they don't need as much attention as an only child.' Write a short essay discussing this sentence, with reference to the special needs of twins.**

Working mothers

Most mothers of children under three want to stay at home. They want their children to have their own special brand of love and individual care. But because they are lonely, a few of them rush back to work. They are likely to be exhausted by two full-time jobs, and unhappy because they feel they are doing neither of them well. Mothers in this situation seem to be getting the worst of both worlds.

This does not apply to mothers with very exciting careers, who earn enough money to pay for highly-experienced and loving mother-substitutes. But these mothers are rare. The average mother returns to a fairly ordinary job with fairly ordinary pay. The other reasons for going back to work are usually the need for extra money; or because the mother does not really enjoy 'mothering' as a full-time job. In these cases, ways must be found to help the mother. If she is forced to stay at home against her will, there is a chance she will build up resentment towards her child.

Points to consider

1 Fathers may well stay at home: they make excellent mother-substitutes and the child has a chance to learn about life through a man's eyes.
2 Grandparents are the most usual source of help. Many a child spends his days happily with Nan or Grandad.
3 State-run nurseries are staffed by qualified nursery nurses. They look after children whose parents are in difficulties.
4 Creches and child-minding facilities are supplied by a few firms. Local councils are considering starting day-care programmes.
5 Private nurseries may be good but are usually expensive. Many mothers cannot afford the payments.
6 Child-minding arose naturally from the need for community self-help. It is now established under the guidance of the social services.

Child-minding

Dreadful stories used to be told about child-minders. They took in too many children, their standard of care was low. Toddlers were found tied to the legs of tables to keep them out of danger, while in other homes terrible accidents happened because the children were neglected. In 1948 an Act of Parliament was passed which stated that all child-minders had to be registered with the social services department of the local council. Since then, child-minding has become very popular. It is a very good way for mothers who do not want to be separated from their own child to earn extra money.

Child-minders must:
(a) be in good health, and have an X-ray if necessary.
(b) have a warm home and enough space for children to play.
(c) have a safe home, with the necessary precautions against fire.
(d) be prepared to provide the children with nourishing food.
(e) keep a register of the children's names and addresses.

(f) never have been convicted of an offence against a child, or had a child taken into care.

(g) allow a social worker to visit their home to check all is going well.

Child-minders are now regarded as doing important work in the community. Many local councils offer them a great deal of help. They hold regular meetings for minders to get together and discuss their work. They run training courses in the needs of small children. They organize visits from the toy library and the playbus (a bus with a specially designed interior where children can play and parents can get advice on and help with the physical, mental, and emotional development of their children). The status of the child-minder has risen enormously. Becoming a child-minder could well be the answer to many a lonely mother's problems.

Questions

1 **Give two reasons why a mother may decide to go back to work before her child is three.**
2 **What might happen if a mother is forced to stay home against her will?**
3 **Where does a mother register to become a child-minder?**
4 **Copy out the seven points required by a person who wishes to become a child-minder.**
5 **In your own words, discuss the importance of child-minding, and the help offered by local councils.**

Helping the balance of the emotions

It must be accepted by parents and others that human life is often difficult. This is because human emotions are complicated, and cause lots of inner conflicts. But saying that life is difficult does not mean that it is 'awful'; rather the opposite. Life is 'awesome', full of magic and mystery as well as inner tensions and fears.

It must also be understood that life is difficult in itself. When the baby frets, the two-year-old explodes with frustration, the six-year-old is anxious and whining, parents need to know these are normal expressions of normal inner conflicts. They are not due to something wrong in the child, or the parents, or the home. (Not, that is, if the child cheers up soon after and reverts to his usual self.)

No matter how much unconditional love is poured into a child, there are bound to be times when he feels 'bad'. The fact that a baby clutches his 'comfort blanket' in such desperate need is a clear demonstration of his feelings of insecurity. Adults have learned to cope with the conflicting tugs of their emotions; a child has not. He needs constant steady reassuring love from parents to guide him through.

Helping the child

1 Parents who accept that life is difficult also accept that their beloved child will have difficult times too.
2 When he is little, they rush to help him. Hunger is urgent in a baby, he cannot cope with his distress.
3 They know the toddler has no control over his feelings. During his 'bad' times they accept his rages will be turned against them.
4 Parents also know that the more successful they are at balancing their own feelings, the more successful a child is likely to be.

Parents have difficulties too

Some parents find it extremely difficult to stay calm and reassuring. They look for other things to blame. They say the child is 'touchy' or 'over-sensitive', that the other parent is 'spoiling' the child, that the child has inherited his grandmother's bad temper, and so on. Parents often find it easier to fly into a fit of temper, or guilt, rather than accept that life is not always as shown in television advertisements.

A parent who feels guilty risks indulging the child; spoiling him by over-doing the loving fuss and sympathy. Once the child learns his rages bring him rewards, he will throw a lot more! He does not learn what he needs to learn: that if parents are not upset, maybe he should not get too upset either.

A parent who gets angry risks intimidating the child – terrifying him by returning rage for rage. This adds outer distress to the child's inner conflicts. He learns that his rages bring him more terror. He becomes afraid of his own

normal bad feelings. He tries to repress (bury) them; he grows nervy, anxious, hostile. It is worth remembering that violence breeds violence. A child is likely to become a bully <u>and</u> a coward if he cannot express unhappy feelings when he is too little to control them.

Points to consider

1 Explosions of frustration are normal and should be ignored. Reacting to them gives them an importance they do not deserve.
2 Calm reassurance – 'you'll feel better in a minute' – helps relieve the child's distress because he trusts parents' wisdom.
3 He learns he <u>can</u> cope, bad feelings are <u>not</u> the end of the world: that soon he will be able to discuss them instead of flying into a rage. This is the beginning of self-control; of learning how to balance the emotions.

Questions

1 **Popular advertisements show babies as smiling and happy. What else must parents accept as a more 'real' picture of childhood life?**
2 **In your own words, explain why parents should not feel guilty or angry when a child flies into a rage.**
3 **Two-year-old Zoe screams and kicks the wall. What might a parent do to help Zoe understand that her panics are not as terrifying as they seem?**
4 **Five-year-old Zack has been sent to his room for fighting. Father unbuckles his belt when he hears toys being thrown about. What advice would you give Zack's father about what Zack really needs to learn?**

Normal problems (1)

What is normal?

Nail-biting used to be thought abnormal. The person chewing his nails was thought to be showing signs of deep inner anxieties. But in a study of fifteen-year-olds in an American school, two-thirds of the teenagers said they used to, or still did, bite their nails. Logic suggests that the one-third who had never bitten their nails were the abnormal ones! This is obviously absurd. Great care must be taken before the words 'normal' and 'abnormal' are used.

What is a problem?

The comfort blanket is common to babies throughout the world. It is used as a defence against anxious feelings that the parent might vanish. This is a perfectly normal anxiety, and the pain of it is quite unbearable. Parents who try to separate a baby from his comfort blanket quickly give it back; the cries of loss are too heart-rending. But while comfort blankets are tolerated, other ways of relieving inner distress are not. Thumbs are pulled out of mouths, fingers are smacked if they touch the genitals, bottoms are beaten if babies prefer the comfort of using their nappies rather than the pot.

1   A normal baby uses anything he can to protect himself against anxiety and unbearable inner conflict.
2   As the child's emotional life develops, so do his ways of getting rid of painful feelings, i.e. his negative emotions.
3   Parents who try to train their child to stop a comfort habit are, in fact, stopping him getting rid of negative emotions.
4   When negative emotions go on too long, the distress turns inward: there are feelings of worthlessness and/or aggressive self-hate.
5   The abnormal child is the one who cannot get rid of his negative emotions. He is so extremely distressed he becomes mentally ill.
6   Fortunately, most babies seem to have good sense about what they need; the thumb is stuck back in the mouth almost as soon as it is pulled out!

Some worries

Children vary, but there are certain behaviour patterns which may show strongly at two, then four, then six. (Though this does not mean that a one, three, or five-year-old has no inner anxieties or conflicts!) The most common worries are: food fads, thumb-sucking, stealing, obsessions, day-dreaming, and lying.

Food fads

Many children develop food fads. One example is suddenly going off milk – really loathing it – and demanding a diet of baked beans and fish fingers. But this new diet is rich in protein, and parents need not worry. When a child refuses one kind of food, he is doing no more than standing up for the rights of the individual and for freedom of choice.

Thumb-sucking

People are constantly putting 'treats' into their mouths: pipe-stems, crisps, fizzy drinks, the end of the biro, loose strands of hair. These 'treats' have very little to do with satisfying hunger. They are comfort habits. Why should a baby be any different? It is now known that some babies suck their thumbs before birth! The harder a parent tries to stop the child, the longer the habit is likely to last. Thumb-sucking stops when the child no longer needs this particular source of comfort; usually well before school.

Questions

1 **In your own words, explain why the words 'normal' and 'abnormal' should not be used without very great care.**
2 **Think of two comfort habits you have. Are they so very different from a small child's?**
3 **Explain why it is important a small child gets rid of his negative emotions.**

Normal problems (2)

Stealing

Stealing is common for a short while: secretly sliding pennies from mother's purse, stealthily hiding father's pen, gives the child a feeling of furtive guilty pleasure. But the pleasure is short-lived because there are painful feelings about stealing. It does not become a comfort habit, so the child soon stops.

However, persistent stealing is a sign the child feels unloved. He tries to gather up parents' possessions to replace what he feels he has lost. Parents should not ignore persistent stealing, but neither should they punish. 'Put the money back, darling, and be quick because I want a cuddle', is positive help. Children will <u>always</u> choose to have parents' affection, rather than stolen goods. When parents truly understand that persistent stealing is stealing back love, they can put things right by <u>putting back love.</u>

Obsessions

Children go through stages of wanting everything just so. They turn into little sergeant-majors; checking the chair is back in its exact place, the spoon and fork aligned by the plate with military precision. If it goes on too long, this obsession with external order can be a sign of inner disorder (muddles and anxieties). The child needs a slower and calmer environment: he needs to develop at his own pace, without too much quickness and hurry.

Day-dreaming

Children have powerful fantasies. They live in very real make-believe worlds which are terrific fun. There are times when a perfectly normal child cannot tell the difference between his two worlds. 'I eated tea with the Queen. She loves my teddy.' If the child spends too long day-dreaming, a parent might say 'What a lovely story. Fetch the crayons and draw me a picture of it.' The child comes back to the real world with the practical problems of fetching crayons and paper, then has to think back to his story-world before he starts drawing. This helps him understand there is a difference in the two worlds, but does not destroy the fun of his fantasy life.

Lying

A balloon bursts with a terrifying bang; then vanishes. The small child cannot make sense of his world: things vanish or shatter when they come near him! For a long while, children cannot accept blame for their actions. 'I never seed it. The lady next door did it,' a child exclaims, gazing at the shattered ruins of a plant pot at his feet. This may seem like the worst kind of lying; but it is the child's natural protection against feelings of anxiety after accidents.

Parents say to a three-year-old 'I think you did pick up the plant. Never mind, let's try to make it better.' The child is much too young to be called 'fibber', or 'liar'.

The straightforward lie 'Yes, I cleaned my teeth' deserves a little frown, nothing more. The child is not practising sly ways. He is protecting himself from parents' disappointment that he forgot to clean his teeth. The small frown is likely to bring on floods of tears; and a quick scramble to the bathroom.

Points to consider

1 Children want their parents' approval; they want to be good.
2 This can be difficult to remember when parents get anxious over what seems like a behaviour problem.
3 But these are the child's natural ways of getting rid of his anxious (negative) feelings, which he cannot control.
4 Lying, stealing and so on need parents' understanding and help. These stages quickly pass if they are treated lightly, with mild disapproval.
5 Slowly, over the years, the child learns to tolerate his anxious feelings. His personality is undamaged by his early experiences of conflict.

Questions

1 **Write a short essay about persistent stealing. What are its causes, and what needs to be done to stop it?**
2 **Children need steady calm environments to develop at their own pace. Give one example of obsessive behaviour in a child whose life is too rushed.**
3 **During the teens, many people have powerful fantasies about their futures. In what ways might fantasies be called comfort habits?**
4 **Explain why it is difficult for a child to accept blame for an accident.**
5 **Adults admit to 'white lies'. Give an example of one, and then compare it with the child who forgot to clean his teeth.**

Punishment or discipline?

Parents who were punished harshly when they were young tend to want to punish their children harshly now. Even when they disagree with the way they were reared, the memory patterns of harsh punishment often break through when they get angry. Little children may be cruelly punished during the egocentric stage – which they cannot help being in! Parents who were treated with compassion and understanding when they were children tend to go for a gentler form of discipline.

Points to consider

1 People like being admired and approved of. Small children are the same.
2 Pleasing parents, making them proud and delighted with his progress, is very important to a small child.
3 Frowns and disappointed looks really do distress a child who is used to loving smiles and lots of approval.
4 They do not work, however, with a child who has become accustomed to angry faces and loud cross voices.
5 Parents who hope to raise their children more gently than they were raised need to remember point 4.
6 Babies cannot be 'naughty'. Parents have to believe this and teach themselves to be gentle and understanding right from the start.

The temper-tantrum stage

By the age of two a small child can be 'naughty' in the adult sense of the word. When he realizes the world is not there to please him, he does his best to control it, to insist on having his own way. He tests his parents' authority, trying to find out how far he can push them – whether they are weaker or stronger than he. He does this by breath-holding, throwing things, lying on the ground and screaming with rage. If this happens in a public place, he usually wins; and no wonder! Many people do not understand how children develop. They think temper tantrums are not normal, that someone must be to blame.

Controlling the child safely through

1 *Firmness:* 'When I say no, darling, I mean no. You understand that.'
2 *Consistency:* 'I said no last time. It's no again this time.'
3 *Calmness:* 'No, Mummy's not cross. Just a bit disappointed.'
4 *Sympathy:* 'Poor darling. It's not nice when I say no, is it?'
5 *Fairness:* 'It hurts my ears when you scream. Scream in another room.'
6 *Reward:* 'That didn't last long. Good boy. Kisses for a good boy.'

Positive control

The above may sound sentimental but it is positive control: the child is learning. His parent will stay firm; she helps him with love through his rages. Her outer control frees him from his own inner confusions and tempers. He feels safe. He stops testing. He gets on with playing and learning.

Negative control

Slaps or threats of no television usually work much more quickly. Parents use these methods when they are too busy for teaching. They are not nearly as helpful to the child when his next rage starts. But negative control is better than no control at all.

Lack of proper control

Children need to learn what is acceptable, and what is unacceptable behaviour. They cannot do this without firm but gentle guidance from parents. An uncontrolled child, or a child who is told off one day and laughed at the next, has real problems with his inner conflicts. He does not grow out of the egocentric stage with time; he must be helped safely through.

Questions

1 **Name two things which distress a child who is raised in a gentle way. From your own observations, do these things upset adults as well?**
2 **Name three things a child does in a temper-tantrum.**
3 **What is meant by positive control? In what ways is it more helpful to a child than negative control?**
4 **Write a short paragraph about lack of proper control.**

Learning about morals and values

Why they are important

The survival of any society depends upon each person being aware of the rights of <u>other</u> people. From adults, this means co-operation, unselfishness, restraint.

A very simple example is the pedestrian crossing. Pedestrians need to know there is one safe place to cross a busy road. All drivers must wait – no matter how much of a hurry they are in. Everybody understands this is fair, and a driver who knocks down a pedestrian on a crossing is severely punished by law. His family and friends are shocked by his selfishness and lack of restraint. He himself will suffer from a guilty conscience at his own behaviour.

The growth of conscience

The development of a conscience is a very subtle business. It is thought a child knows right from wrong by the age of seven. He has developed some idea of order, fair play and justice. He has developed ideas of personal honour and personal pride. This means he tries to behave well not simply to please others, but for his own inner sense of personal satisfaction. At this young age, he makes many mistakes; but then, so do adults. He needs to be praised for his successes, and quickly forgiven the rest. The growth of conscience is a tremendous step forward in his development as an individual.

Teaching by example

Parents teach children by their actions, more than by their words.

Parents teach children by their actions, more than by their words.

Like all other teaching, moral values are first learned at home. The child learns by example and imitation, not by words. Some parents tell children one thing, then promptly do the opposite. If a child watches his mother stealing, he <u>cannot</u> believe he should not copy – even though she may tell him not to. Parents 'teach' children by their <u>actions</u>, more than by their words.

Good manners

Eating in the street used to be thought 'bad manners' or 'rude'. Nowadays, most parents do not mind at all. But like most good manners, it had a basis of common sense. There was no sanitation; dropped food could be covered in humans' mess. Nowadays, a dropped sweet can pick up some of the lead from the exhaust of motor-cars, or be covered in dogs' mess. Lead is damaging to the child's growing brain; there may be worms in the dogs' faeces which cause serious diseases in children.

Good manners need to have a basis of sound common sense to do with the welfare of other people as well as the welfare of the child. Like the teaching of moral values, the child learns how to behave from following parents' <u>example</u>, rather than what they say.

Questions

1 **Name four ideas a child must develop to know right from wrong.**
2 **Why do you think it important he tries to behave well for his own personal satisfaction? This is not a simple question. You may need a class discussion before you answer.**
3 **Where are moral values first learned? In what ways does the child learn them?**
4 **Good manners should have a basis of sound common sense. Would you (a) allow a child to leave the lavatory door open if he is frightened, (b) shut it sternly and leave him there to cry, (c) go inside with him till he gets over his fears?**
5 **Which of these three would you correct in a seven-year-old: (a) putting elbows on the table, (b) eating with his mouth open, (c) snatching food from a younger child's plate? Try to give reasons for your answer.**

Aggression and co-operation

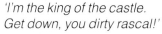

*'I'm the king of the castle.
Get down, you dirty rascal!'*

*'Three blind mice, three blind mice.
See how they run, see how they run.
They all run after the farmer's wife
Who cut off their tails with the carving knife.'*

Aggression

Aggression is the natural urge to fight for what is wanted. It is also the need to dominate: to be 'king of the castle'. Aggressive feelings are common to everyone, though they seem stronger in some children than in others. Parents automatically stop a child who is being cruel to any thing or person smaller and weaker; this is absolutely essential. A child showing aggression is not necessarily going to turn into a bully: he may be practising skills of courage and determination. But aggression alarms some parents: 'I'll beat him senseless,' they say aggressively, determined to stamp it out of the child!

Children need to get rid of their aggression in fairly harmless ways. Beating up teddy and kicking the wall are natural things to do. It is not yet known whether aggression is stronger in boys than in girls, and whether parents are partly responsible or not. But little girls may attack by name-calling and spiteful teasing, whereas little boys punch and kick in actual fights.

The more outgoing and sociable a child is, the more aggression he is bound to show in each different situation. The strong urge to aggressive behaviour can be checked by <u>gentle</u> example at home, and by appeals to the child's growing desire to help and protect.

The urge to help and protect

Altruism is the natural urge to help and protect. A six-month-old baby seeing his mother laugh may begin laughing too, though he was in the middle of tears. Crying in response to a parent's crying can start before the age of one. Human emotions are infectious: they are highly catching. They pass between people like gleaming rainbows – or like vicious germs.

At two, the plight of the three blind mice can bring tears to a child's eyes. 'Poor mices wiv no eyses. Horble lady cut off tails. Cut lady off.' At three, the urge to help and protect is beginning to emerge. 'Poor mices go to doctor, make better. Me look after mices.' A four-year-old child seeing a worm uncovered, crouches down and covers it gently with earth, murmuring sympathetic noises.

The child also develops a need to help even where there is no distress: 'Me get Daddy's slippers', 'Me take care of Mummy'. Parents are enchanted by these sympathetic actions – their wilful aggressive egocentred child is finally becoming civilized. They should not be too dismayed if, the next day, the child digs up the worm and stamps on it – 'deaded!'

There is no difference in the sexes in the slow development of altruistic feelings; boys are as tender and loving and caring as girls.

Points to consider

1 The urge to help, to protect, to relieve distress, develops slowly as the child fights inner battles between aggression and altruism.
2 Both altruism and aggression have their proper place in human emotions.
3 The tough of sixteen who joins with his gang in attacking an old man may have natural feelings of sympathy for the victim, which he hides because he is a coward: 'afraid of peer-group power'.
4 The bountiful lady who hands out money and talks in reverent tones about 'the poor' may have no real sympathy at all.
5 Children learn from parents' example and gentle control that there is a proper balance in what may seem like two opposite emotions; e.g. you do not kill the farmer's wife (extreme aggression) or risk your own life (extreme altruism). You do protect the weak and helpless with all the courage you possess.

Questions

1 **What is meant by 'aggression'? What is meant by 'altruism'?**
2 **Is it natural for children to be aggressive? Give reasons for your answer.**
3 **Write a short essay explaining why parents should remember that human emotions are highly infectious.**
4 **A child is beaten senseless for his violent behaviour. Do you think he learns more about (a) altruism or (b) aggression? Why?**
5 **If parents have a row in front of a child, does it help more if they kiss and make-up (a) in private or (b) in front of the child? Give reasons for your answer.**

The average five-year-old

By the time the child is about five, half his intellectual growth is over. This seems as amazing as the fact that his brain is almost 90% of its adult weight. Many five-year-olds do not read or write. They have at least ten years of studying ahead – for some people It could be twenty years. Below is a list of some of the things a child has learned before he starts school.

Says his full name, his age, and his home address.
Speaks fluently in proper sentences with good grammar.
Dresses and undresses himself, though he may need help with shoe laces.
Goes to the toilet alone; washes and dries hands afterwards.
Listens to simple instructions and then carries them out.
Takes part in conversations which he finds interesting.
Understands the need for rules and fair play.
Chooses his own friends and makes up games with them.
Protects and looks after younger children and pets.
Comforts his friends when they are upset.
Names four colours and is able to match others he cannot name.
Recognizes and writes a few letters of the alphabet.
Has some idea of time, and the days of the week.
Uses pencils, crayons, paintbrush, to make simple pictures.

Ready for school?

Many people can still remember their first weeks at school with terror. The child is taken from his familiar home to a huge strange place. He is separated from his mother and handed into the care of an unknown person (the class teacher). He is put in a room with thirty or more other strange children. He may be terrified his mother has left him there for ever. Or something quite small might upset him: at home he washes hands before lunch, not after – or the other way around.

Preparing for school

The child should visit the school the term before he starts. He is shown around the room; sits at a desk; looks at the pictures. He sees his parent chatting in a friendly way to the teacher. At home, the new clothes for school are bought early so he gets used to trying them on. School lunches are explained so he knows what to expect. Parents tell stories of their own first days at school (ending happily). Play-acting games of standing-in-line, answering-the-register help school to sound fun and not too unfamiliar.

The first term

1   The child must have all the equipment he needs. This gives him confidence. Later on, parents may have to skimp, but not when he is very young.
2   The child's clothes and equipment must be clearly labelled. His home address should be on the inside of his school bag or jacket.

3   He needs to recognize his name on the labels. If he cannot read his name, a special mark he can 'read' should be inked on near his name.
4   In the early morning he needs enough time not to be rushed and hurried. Arriving at school calmly is the best start to his day.
5   A parent should stay with an anxious child for as long as the teacher and/or parent thinks it is necessary.

Questions

1   **From the list of things an average five-year-old can do:**
    (a)   name three things which show the child's social development.
    (b)   name two things which show his physical development.
    (c)   name six things which show his mental development.
2   **In your own words, explain why a child might be very frightened during his first weeks at school.**
3   **Write down four ways in which you would help a child prepare his mind and emotions for school.**
4   **Why do you think it helps for a child to start his morning calmly?**

From five to seven

The five-year-old does not easily join in school activities; not at first. He stands and watches, as if sizing up the situation, learning these strange new ways of behaviour. Small children holding hands in a singing game look and sound terribly wooden. There is no <u>obvious</u> joy as there is in their unstructured play at home. They are being introduced to the next stage of social life: organization of large numbers of people belonging in the same peer group – structured work and play.

1   The life of school forces a child further along the road to independence.
2   He receives many shocks: five- and six-year-olds prefer to play in groups of two.
3   The child's fantasy (make-believe) world is torn apart when facts are insisted upon. He may be called a 'fibber' when he tells his 'stories'.
4   He may be picked upon and tormented by the other children for no apparent reason – this is not unusual, but is quickly spotted by a good teacher.
5   He faces real competition: no matter how excellent the teacher, she cannot give equal attention to all the children, all the time.

The child from a satisfactory home is ready for these challenges. He wants and needs organized games and structured learning, which he cannot get at home. He is ready for his world to be widened, which is the aim of education. It is the child from an unsatisfactory home who is likely to find school disappointing. His need for a close personal relationship is stronger than his need to learn. As his secret hopes of teacher replacing mother fade, he may become extremely disruptive, or extremely withdrawn. The teacher asks the parents to visit school so things can be put right. If this fails, she may seek help from the Child Guidance Clinic.

At home

1   Home life needs to be steady while the child adjusts to school.
2   A time of bed-wetting, needing a light at night, being terrified of dogs, stepping on the cracks in pavements, imagining a harmless old person is evil, may be quite normal.
3   Parents may blame the school for these fears, but they are natural. It is better the child feels secure enough to show them, than that he represses (buries) them, for fear his parents 'give teacher a piece of their mind'.
4   Some mothers go back to work once the child has settled at school. This does not harm the child, providing someone is there to care for him when he arrives home: older siblings, a neighbour, a grandparent.
5   When the child begins the 'teacher says' sort of boasting, parents can know the child has settled well.

People who help

1   The education welfare officer checks on school attendance. Frequent non-attendance of small children often means problems at home.
2   The educational psychologist at the Child Guidance Centre (see pp. 186–7) tests a child's mental and emotional development. This gives parents and teachers a clearer understanding of the child's special needs.
3   The school nurse, dentist, and doctor check on the child's physical health some time during his first year. Problems of speech, sight, hearing, and so on, will be picked up then, if the child has not been taken for his developmental checks when younger.

Questions

1   **Name two ways a five-year-old is likely to behave when he starts school.**
2   **Describe three of the shocks a child is likely to receive.**
3   **In your own words, explain why adjusting to school may be extremely difficult for a child from an unsatisfactory home.**
4   **Does a normal happy child suffer fears at around this time?**
5   **What is the work of the educational psychologist? Why is it important?**
6   **What would you say to a parent who refused to take a pre-school child for developmental checks because 'If anything's wrong, they'll find it out when he starts school'?**

Further work on Chapter 6

1   Visit a nursery for the under-twos. Ask the staff about their training and their work. Write a paragraph describing a nursery nurse's job.

2   Visit a Mother and Toddler group. Write a short essay on what you observed of a child's need to be close to his mother.

3   At a Pre-school Playgroup, observe children's quarrels, and the way they are resolved. Write down all the ways in which arguments (a) can be avoided and (b) can best be sorted out happily.

4   Describe a temper tantrum you have seen. Make notes on (a) the child's behaviour and (b) the adult's reactions.

5   At the age of sixteen you can visit your local magistrates' or county court. If possible, watch a case involving a minor breach of the law. Write an essay explaining the importance of teaching a small child morals and values.

6   Visit the town planning office for information on the work of town planners, with reference to the needs of small children, e.g. high-rise buildings, ring roads, new towns, lack of play space. If you live in a rural area, ask the local education officer to give a talk on problems arising in families which are isolated.

7   Write an essay describing the advantages and disadvantages of raising a child in (a) a crowded city and (b) an isolated village.

8   Write down your own ideas about what you consider is the most suitable sized family. Then explain why you have chosen that particular number of children, using evidence from your own childhood and from others you have observed.

9   After careful observation, make notes on the development of protective feelings you have seen in any one particular child.

10 Imagine you are three months old. Would you prefer to have parents who love you conditionally, or unconditionally? Give reasons for your answer.

11 'Parents should not make comparisons between siblings.' Do you agree, or disagree? Discuss this with special reference to the child's feelings.

12 At your playgroup, play games with a child who is starting school next term. Check his progress against the list of skills an average five-year-old has developed.

13 (a) How might a five-year-old react to going to school if he has been largely kept at home until that time?
         Suggest ways of preparing a child for going to school.
    (b) Give advice to a mother whose three-year-old child has temper tantrums when they are out shopping. Why might the child behave in this way?   (SREB)

14 Write fully on the advantages of the following to the social and emotional development of a child:
    (a) grandparents
    (b) brothers and/or sisters.   (WMEB)

Chapter 7

Children with special needs

Deaf children enjoying school.

Handicap and disability

Sadly, a few babies are born with more than one disability. But for the purpose of this study, handicaps are discussed in three separate sections.

1 Physical handicap – the <u>body</u> is disabled in some way.
2 Mental handicap – the <u>mind</u> is disabled in some way.
3 Emotional handicap – the <u>emotions</u> are disabled in some way.

A handicap may be very severe; the baby is very disabled. Or a handicap may be quite mild; the baby is only slightly disabled. Whether the handicap is severe or mild, the baby is a human person needing human love like all other babies. Handicapped babies used to be locked away in institutions. Nowadays, parents are encouraged to care for their babies at home. This is not always easy. Parents need a great deal of help and support to raise their baby. Often, the people around the child react so negatively that what was a mild disability soon turns into a severe problem. This also works the other way around: positive reactions help a severely disabled child to do much better than would have been expected.

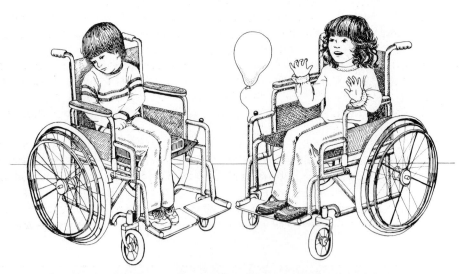

Zoe is born with mild cerebral palsy. She cannot control her limbs or her movements. Zoe's parents are terribly upset. They back away from Zoe as if she is a fearful monster. The doctor, midwife, and health visitor explain the illness in great detail. Zoe's parents listen, and gradually get over their shock. They take Zoe home; she becomes one of the family. Zoe's mother has a dreadful time with the neighbours, but she is supported by her husband and loving grandparents. Zoe has an active mind and a loving nature. Her parents know she will always be physically backward compared with other children. But they are not interested in comparison: they love Zoe dearly and take great delight in each slight step of her very slow development.

Zack is also born with mild cerebral palsy. His parents react in exactly the same way as Zoe's. But the staff at the hospital are not good at dealing with upset parents. They explain Zack's illness, but his parents cannot accept what they say. They rush Zack home; they hide him from family and neighbours. They do their best for him, but they cannot bring themselves to be fond of him. Zack, tucked away in a back room with nothing to interest his mind and no one to love him, grows into a child with many other problems. He becomes mentally backward and emotionally disturbed.

Zack's parents cannot help their feelings: nor can the staff at the hospital and the health visitor. Many people have deep fears about handicap. They are primitive feelings: it takes a long time to grow out of them. Zack's parents do not deliberately set out to make Zack's life even more difficult; nor do the medical staff set out to be callous or cruel. Zoe is lucky in that the people close to her have exceptional moral strengths, and depths of human loving kindness.

It is important to understand that primitive fears about handicap can be very powerful indeed. Some people would argue that Zoe should be 'put down like an animal' because she will be a terrible burden on her parents, and on the state. Has Zoe committed a crime by being born less-than-perfect? Who are these 'perfect' people who would condemn her to death? Have they no flaws themselves?

1 Handicap can happen in any family, to any kind of parents.
2 It is usually no one's fault: not inherited nor caused by the environment.
3 People, especially parents, should try not to think in terms of blame or fault. Sadly, now and then, these things just happen.
4 But if there is a history in the family of a certain inherited illness, parents can get advice from the genetic counselling services before they plan their families.
5 It is not unusual to feel repelled by a less-than-perfect baby.
6 Parents need lots of time to cope with these feelings: to get over their sense of loss for the perfect baby they longed for.
7 They need real help from the state: enough money, a great deal of nursing aid, plenty of support so they do not become overwhelmed with exhaustion.
8 Their task is more heroic than climbing the highest mountain. Climbers want to test their endurance for a short time; they do it for fun. Parents raise their handicapped children from the highest human motives. There is no time limit on their endurance; they are the world's greatest unsung heroines and heroes.

Questions

1 **Copy out the three separate ways in which handicap will be studied.**
2 **What do all babies need, whether handicapped or not?**
3 **'That baby's hardly human. Poor you!' exclaims a neighbour. Explain how damaging this negative kind of sympathy can be to parents.**
4 **'Her eyes are beautiful. Look, she's smiling!' exlaims another neighbour. Explain why this positive attitude is so important to the handicapped baby, and to the parents.**
5 **Have a discussion on whether severely disabled babies should be destroyed at birth. Try to ignore your own inner impulses (subjective reactions) and look at the question objectively. Make notes on whether the debate centres around money or ethics.**
6 **Name at least three things parents need in their struggle to raise a handicapped child.**

Congenital disability

Congenital means 'present at birth'. Sadly, some disabilities happen for which there is no known cause. Cerebral palsy, which damages the part of the brain controlling movement, can happen in any family and for no obvious reason. However, the causes of many disabilities are now known. Some can be detected in the early life of the foetus. Some can be prevented by the pregnant mother having good antenatal care. Couples with serious inherited diseases need not start a baby if they decide the risk is too great (p. 51).

Causes of congenital disability

1   Inherited diseases are passed on the genes or chromosomes of the parents (p. 60). A dominant gene carries the risk of one in two children being affected. Two recessive genes carry the risk of one in four children having the disease.
(a) Some black Americans and Africans suffer from sickle-cell anaemia, which is a weakness in the red blood cells. Thalassaemia is a similar disease of some people in Mediterranean countries. These are serious anaemias and mothers who are affected need very special care during their pregnancy. Their children also require very special care.
(b) Severe spina bifida happens in one in every 500 births. It is a malformation of the spine which can affect the nerves and cause paralysis (no movement). It is thought many genes may be involved and other external factors as well.
Spina bifida can be detected by blood tests followed by amniocentesis (p. 52).
(c) Haemophilia is a rare disease which stops the blood clotting. It is carried on the sex chromosomes and passed from mothers to sons. Colour-blindness is also sex-linked, which means women rarely suffer from it – about 8 per cent of men do.
(d) Down's Syndrome is not an inherited disease, though it is caused by faulty chromosomes (p. 183).

2   Diseases such as rubella (German measles) affect the baby while it is in the womb. Rubella in early pregnancy can cause severe damage to the heart, brain, eyes, and inner ear of the foetus. Rubella is now prevented by girls having the disease or being immunized against it before puberty. Other damaging diseases include syphilis and gonorrhoea (p. 38). The health of the mother during pregnancy is very important as it is now thought more ordinary illnesses such as chicken-pox can affect the foetus too.

3   External factors are things which can put the baby 'at risk' of damage. They include such things as diet (p. 49), smoking, drinking, and drugs (p. 46).
(a) Irradiation caused by atomic explosion caused severe mental handicap in babies born to mothers at Hiroshima and Nagasaki in Japan during the Second World War. Irradiation from X-rays is also damaging (p. 47).
(b) The age of the mother can affect the foetus. The older the mother, the greater the risk of Down's Syndrome, mental handicap, poor physical development, and premature labour. Older fathers too are linked with certain kinds of poor development of the foetus.
(c) 'Close parity' means having babies close together. Mothers and babies are likely to have safer pregnancies if there is a gap of two years between births.

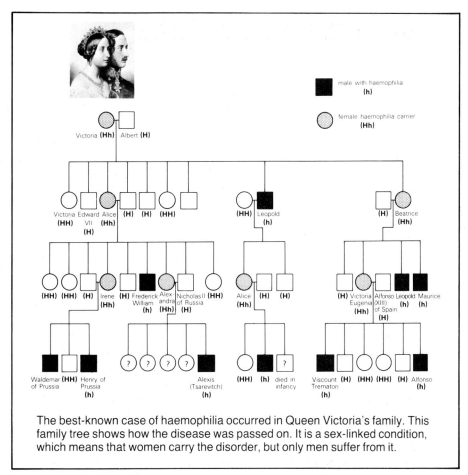

The best-known case of haemophilia occurred in Queen Victoria's family. This family tree shows how the disease was passed on. It is a sex-linked condition, which means that women carry the disorder, but only men suffer from it.

(d) Big upheavals such as changing jobs, moving house, death in the family, or divorce are called life-crises. Mothers who suffer five or more life-crises during pregnancy may have less well-developed babies.

(e) Unsupported mothers without loving husbands often suffer financial, social and emotional distress. Their babies may not do as well as babies born to mothers who have planned their families with the support of a husband and the safety of a home.

External factors do not <u>necessarily</u> mean the baby will be damaged (apart from irradiation!) and mothers in these situations should not become worried. They are listed here so that people have the information to make sensible choices about their life-styles. Many parents want to know, for example, whether to have their babies close together or to space them out. On the other hand, these same parents may well come from families where perfectly healthy babies were born within twelve months of one another.

Questions

1 **What is meant by 'congenital disability'?**
2 **Name two inherited diseases.**
3 **Write a short description of rubella and explain how it can be prevented.**
4 **What is meant by 'external factors'? Explain in what ways knowing about them can be useful for people planning their families.**

Physically disabled children

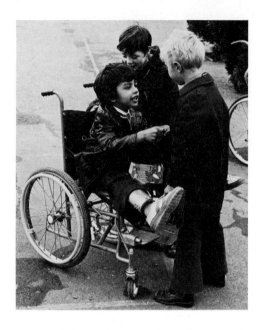

A child born with a defect such as a cleft palate and lip looks far more damaged than he actually is. The bones which did not join together can be repaired by surgery. Some other defects such as dislocated hips or under-developed limbs are also immediately noticed, and the correct medical help is given.

Other defects do not always show up immediately. Problems with eye-sight or hearing need further testing when the baby reaches the average milestones for following a moving object with his eyes and turning his head in the direction of sounds. Even then, the doctor may not be able to decide whether there is something wrong, or whether the baby is simply not interested in doctors and their tests! Parents need to remember this: it can help cut down the agony of waiting. Speech defects will not show up until much later, but by two, the child should be saying a few words.

The importance of regular check-ups

Parents are told at the end of each visit when to bring the child in for the next check-up. Regular appointments are very important. A physical defect does not always show up immediately. The sooner it is noticed, the sooner the child can receive the required treatment. A defect which is not noticed until the child starts school is likely to cause much more serious problems of mental and emotional development. For example: after severe earache, a one-year-old may become slightly deaf. As he cannot hear words, his speech development stops. He becomes frustrated because no one understands his problems. He turns from being a happy lively child into a sullen, aggressive five-year-old: backward because he cannot learn; and disruptive or withdrawn.

It is essential a fully-trained medical person tests all children's developmental progress until the age of five to seven.

How the child feels about his disability

Babies do not know they have defects. They learn about them as they grow. They learn from their parents and family; later, they learn from comparing themselves with other children. It is the early stage of learning which affects the child most.

No one wants to be thought of with pity. Pity robs people of their self-respect, and their will to go on trying. Parents have to be careful not to become too over-protective. The physically disabled child needs to be encouraged, and then encouraged again, to keep on trying. A child who is unable to walk cannot explore for himself. He cannot follow parents around, and learn by copying what they are doing. But he can be strapped into a home-made buggy with a rope attached and pull himself about: he can learn to operate a motorized cart. 'Open the door for me,' Mum says, as she picks up a heavy-laden tray. The child's face beams with pride: his help is needed, he is not a useless drag on the family.

Points to consider

1 A child who has something wrong with his body is called physically disabled, not handicapped.
2 This makes it quite clear the child is perfectly normal, apart from his disability – which is ignored as much as possible.
3 He needs encouragement and help to develop all the abilities he has – the things he can do.
4 A physiotherapist is a person trained in special exercises which improve physical skills, or which stop the disability getting worse.
5 An occupational therapist gives advice on suitable games and toys to occupy the child until he is ready for school.
6 A disabled child has special educational needs, but, if it is possible, he will be encouraged to attend ordinary schools.
7 This is because he also needs to be part of the community, and to have plenty of people his own age to play with.
8 At times, he is likely to feel a bit depressed as there are so many exciting things he cannot do.
9 He needs masses of love from cheerful, matter-of-fact parents; he needs jokes and good company from his school friends.
10 His parents need a great deal of extra support: people to help with the shopping or laundry, or to take the child out so they can have some rest.

Questions

1 **Explain why an eye defect is not always noticed at birth.**
2 **Write a full essay, showing that you understand the importance of regular check-ups on the child's physical health.**
3 **Explain why pity is a negative reaction to a child with a disability.**
4 **Name two people who can give the child extra help and say what they do.**
5 **Why is a child with special educational needs encouraged to attend ordinary schools?**

Mentally handicapped children

Bennett House Special School, Abingdon.

A child who is very slow indeed at learning is called mentally handicapped. He is behind other children in his level of understanding: he has a handicap of the mind. This does not necessarily mean there is anything wrong; just that his mind works at a much slower pace than other children's. When he arrives at school, he will be tested to find out his intelligence quotient, his IQ. This is not easy; he may be too backward for a proper assessment.

1 The average child's IQ is 100.
2 A child with an IQ between 50 and 70 is educationally subnormal (mild), ESN.
3 A child with an IQ below 50 is educationally subnormal (severe), SSN.
4 Both groups of children can learn school subjects, but they must be taught at a much slower rate.
5 Special schools have staff trained to help with learning difficulties.
6 The number of children in each class is much lower than in ordinary schools.

Children from homes where there is little stimulation are likely to be backward. And children from homes in great emotional upset are often too disturbed to learn, and need the help of a special school. It is easy for the staff at a child clinic to spot a severely mentally handicapped baby. But the child who is only mildly subnormal may not be noticed until he arrives at school. Parents get a great shock: they think special schools are terrible places. They are not. They give the child the special separate attention he so desperately needs, and which he would not be able to get in a crowded class of infants.

Known causes for mental handicap

Damage to the brain cells during pregnancy or labour is one of the main causes for mental handicap, where something has gone wrong. In severe cases of cerebral palsy, the damage to the brain spreads to the 'thinking' parts as well. During a few births, lack of oxygen from mother to baby can kill off many brain cells. There are other conditions too which can damage the baby's delicate brain. Once brain cells are destroyed they cannot be mended or replaced like other cells: the damage is permanent. Labour wards have oxygen and special drugs ready, just in case. Mothers who have had difficult births in the past and first-time mothers usually feel safer about their baby's health if he is delivered in hospital.

Down's Syndrome (mongol children)

This condition is caused by an extra chromosome in the cells: 47 instead of 46. It is not clear why this happens. Older mothers of 35+ are more at risk. They are offered amniocentesis (testing the amniotic fluid) for Down's Syndrome, and they may choose to terminate their pregnancy if the results are positive.

All Down's babies are mentally handicapped, some more mildly than others. Mental handicap makes the baby physically backward too, as it takes him much longer to learn to look after himself. But the children can be loving and affectionate, with placid cheerful natures. This may be partly due to the fact that parents do not put pressure on them to 'do well'. A Down's baby is easily recognized by his rather small eyes which slant, and his flat short nose. Down's Syndrome is not curable, but the children learn to walk not long after normal children, and many do quite well at special schools.

Malnutrition

In under-developed countries, malnutrition is often the greatest cause of mental handicap. During the last weeks of pregnancy and the first three years of life the baby's brain can be damaged by lack of proper nourishment. This is the time of the greatest growth spurt of the brain and a good diet, rich in protein foods, is essential. It is tragic to think of small children lost in mindless confusion, when all they needed was enough milk and a good diet to become bright lively youngsters.

Questions

1   **Write down the average child's IQ, and then that of the ESN and the SSN child. Learn them.**
2   **Explain the difference between ESN and SSN.**
3   **Give reasons why it is better for a mentally handicapped child to attend a special school, rather than the local infants' school.**
4   **Write a short description of a Down's Syndrome child: his appearance and temperament.**

Emotionally disturbed children

A child is at risk of becoming disturbed when his emotional (inner) life is so frightful that he cannot 'pay attention' to the outside world. His fears for his safety threaten to overwhelm him. His inner conflicts become too painful to bear. He stops learning, and this is hardly surprising: people in great pain concentrate on waiting for the agony to stop. The small child lacks even this crumb of comfort. He has no notion of time. He has no notion that things might get better.

Locked into this terrifying place – this hell on earth – he does the one thing left. He retreats from it: he withdraws into himself. He does not do this consciously, by thinking about it. His agonized little mind is simply trying to avoid more pain. A child cut off from society does not develop normal patterns of behaviour. His disturbed emotions stay disturbed, whether he becomes disruptive or withdrawn. He needs urgent help from the Child Guidance Centre.

Emotional disturbance in a child cannot be diagnosed (decided) by an untrained person. It is caused by a wide variety of different things. One of the main reasons is lack of understanding by parents. This usually happens when parents are trapped in their own inner conflicts, and need help.

Unrealistic expectations

Something which is unrealistic does not 'fit' the situation. Unrealistic expectations mean that parents have unreal ideas about how they expect a child to be.

Examples of unrealistic expectations
The mother dreams of a sweet gurgly baby without understanding that he will be a dirty noisy baby too. She is so disappointed, she keeps away from him as much as possible. The father dreams of a son just like him without understanding the child is bound to be different because of his inherited mixture of genes. He turns harsh and over-critical, trying to force the child's character to be more like his own.

Lack of empathy

An empathetic person can imagine how it feels to <u>be</u> another person. Parents who lack empathy for a helpless infant cannot help the child, usually because their own problems are too distressing.

Examples of lack of empathy

The mother who refuses to comfort her weeping child because she is afraid of spoiling him – but is <u>not</u> afraid of his obvious distress. The father who throws a two-year-old in the deep end of the pool because he is afraid the child will be a cissy – but is <u>not</u> afraid of nearly drowning him.

Role reversal

Role reversal means turning a situation the other way around. This happens when parents use the child as if he were 'parent' to them; they want comfort and love <u>from</u> the child, instead of giving it to him.

Examples of role reversal

Parents start a baby to patch up their broken marriage; expecting a baby to do what they themselves have failed at. A seven-year-old is kept home from school to keep mother company. Father plays flirting games with his daughter; but sees his son as a threat to his manhood.

Belief in punishment

Belief in punishment, rather than teaching by example and gentle discipline, comes from hidden terrors and cruelties buried deep within the parent. Children are seen as wild animals who have to be broken-in like beasts.

Examples of belief in punishment

The mother who locks a small child in a dark cupboard and slams the front door, pretending to leave the child alone there for ever. The father who beats the child suddenly and with great violence or, even more cruelly, makes the child wait in quaking terror for hours before the promised beating.

Questions

1 **Why does a disturbed child cut himself off from the outer world?**
2 **What is meant by 'unrealistic expectations'? Give one example.**
3 **What is meant by 'lack of empathy'?**
4 **What is meant by 'role reversal'? Copy out or make up one example of your own.**
5 **Write a paragraph explaining your own opinions on 'belief in punishment'.**

Putting things right

From generation unto generation . . .

It is likely the parents of disturbed children had very unhappy childhoods themselves. As there was no teaching of Child Development when they grew up, they repeated the same terrible patterns with their own children – without knowing why. Parents start off wanting to be as loving and caring as they can possibly be. It is when the responsibilities of parenthood have to be faced that the buried pains and unresolved conflicts from their own childhoods break through.

The future?

It is important to remember that human patterns of behaviour can change. People who had very sad childhoods need to give themselves time as adults to work through their unhappy early experiences, before starting their own families. Babies are not the answer to a young girl's loneliness. The demands of small children can drive an unhappy couple even further apart. People with sad childhoods often long for a baby to heal their terrible wounds. This is quite natural: they ache with so much love they could not properly share with their own parents. If they make a success of marriage with all its ups and downs, they can be reassured they will make a success of parenthood too.

Points to consider

1 People who had sad childhoods can make the very best of parents.
2 They have learned, through their own experience, what makes a child happy or unhappy.
3 No parents are perfect. Raising children is very demanding emotionally, and all parents make mistakes from time to time.
4 Parents need to understand they can get their lives into frightful muddles without damaging their children.
5 The damage done to a disturbed child is emotional, and comes from cold, unloving, unfeeling, and over-critical parents.
6 Social conditions such as poor housing, unemployment, lack of money, put very great pressures on parents struggling to raise their children.
7 But many a child is damaged physically, as well as emotionally, in homes where parents have secure jobs and plenty of money.
8 A child who is loved unconditionally will develop well, no matter what his parents' background or income.

The Child Guidance Centre

Things can go wrong in a child's development for which parents are not responsible. A child may be referred to the Child Guidance Centre by the health visitor, the social worker, the teacher, the doctor; or the parents themselves can ask for help. At the centre, the child is assessed (checked) to find out what is causing his disturbed behaviour. Parents may be told the problem has a medical cause.

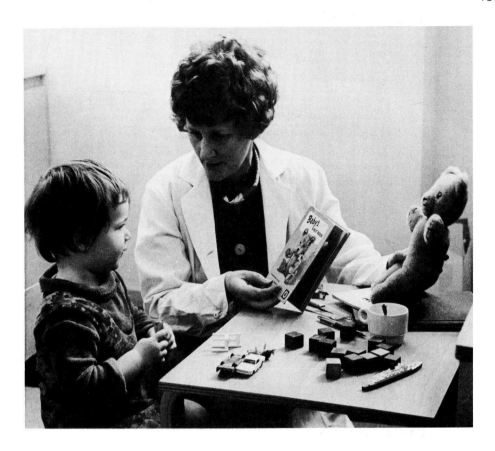

It is important parents attend the centre, whatever the cause of the child's problems. The staff know child-rearing is difficult. They are not looking for fault or blame. They are trained to help put things right; which parents long for, but may be too embarrassed to ask. The idea of 'natural' parenting being easy dies hard in people's minds. This is sad because it stops parents going for help when they need it. Parents should feel that they can use the Child Guidance Centre in much the same was as they use the clinic or Child Health Centre.

Questions

1 **'Parents start off wanting to be loving . . .' In your own words, explain why things sometimes go wrong.**
2 **Write a full essay, discussing the ways in which unhappiness need not be passed on from generation unto generation.**
3 **Explain the role of the Child Guidance Centre.**

Children adrift

People get into difficulties, and so do families. Changing attitudes towards divorce and illegitimacy convince some parents that it is easy to raise children alone. (Of the one in six babies conceived outside marriage, only half end up with married parents.) But it is not easy to raise children without a partner's support. Many single parents break down under the strain and ask to put their children into care. In cases of non-accidental injury (baby battering) and parents' neglect, the local authorities have a duty to remove the child from danger. But the most usual reasons for children being put in care are sudden illness or family crisis.

No child should feel unwanted or unloved. Having people he belongs to is as important to his development as the air he breathes. About half the children in care are looked after by 'house-parents' in children's homes. (The modern names for anyone looking after a child are 'caregiver' and 'caretaker'.) Social workers try to place as many children as possible in ordinary homes, because the small cosy unit of the family suits a child better.

A children's home in Wolverhampton.

Adoption

1 Adoption is the acceptance of a child by parent-substitutes who then legally become the child's rightful parents.
2 The duties and rights of the natural parents are permanently taken over by the adoptive parents, and the child takes their name.

3   The child usually loses ties with his natural parents, though older adopted children may keep up ties with a responsible loving relative.
4   In Britain, about half a million children have been adopted over the past fifty years. The peak year was 1968, with 27,000 adoptions.
5   The number of babies available for adoption has dropped dramatically. This may be due to contraception and abortion, also less worry about illegitimacy.
6   People who wish to adopt should consider children with special needs, black children, and much older children, who long for homes of their own with loving parents.

Fostering

1   Fostering is also called 'boarding out'. This shows the child is not permanently separated from his own family.
2   Many children need only short-stay fostering while the parent recovers from childbirth, an illness, or whatever crisis has arisen.
3   Some foster parents look after disabled children to allow parents a much-needed break for a couple of weeks.
4   In long-stay fostering, the natural parents hope to keep in touch, but many are in such acute personal difficulties they lose contact, which is very distressing for the child.
5   In England and Wales, the figures for 1979 show that of the 100,100 children in local authority care about 36,000 were boarded out and another 19,000 were estimated to be in private foster homes.
6   Fostering is an alternative to residential nurseries and children's homes. More places are needed for older children, and children with special needs.

Points to consider

1   Adoption is more successful than fostering as the child is likely to make the close loving ties essential for healthy emotional development.
2   But fostering is the answer to many distressed parents' needs: they hope to bring the child home again just as soon as they have their own problems sorted out.

Books to read

Children who wait J. Rowe & L. Lambert, ABAA 1973
The receiving end N. Timms, Routledge & Kegan Paul 1973
Adoption of non-white children L. Raynor, Allen & Unwin 1971
Born illegitimate E. Crelling, M. Kellmer Pringle, P. West, NFER 1971

Questions

1   **Give two reasons why well-loved children may be put in short-stay care.**
2   **Why do social workers try to place children in ordinary homes?**
3   **Nowadays, it is older children and children with special needs who hope for adoption or fostering. Can you think of any reasons why this is so?**
4   **Write a short essay, clearly explaining the difference between adoption and fostering.**

Child abuse (baby-battering)

Child abuse: a cigarette burn and (*right*) skin raw from continuous beatings.

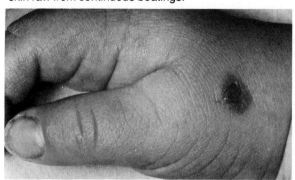

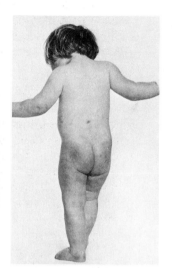

Once a baby is born, parents lose their personal freedom. Another life now depends on them. They cannot dash off when the whim suddenly takes them. They must stop and consider the baby's needs as well. This loss of personal freedom comes as a great shock to a few parents. Sadly, they react very violently indeed. They punish the baby for existing. They are too immature to accept responsibility for the human life they have created.

1 Child abuse includes deaths, serious or moderate battering, and failure to thrive (the baby stops growing due to neglect).
2 The British Paediatric (child) Association estimates that child abuse is the fourth commonest cause of death in children under five.
3 In the first year of life, 400 cases of babies with brain damage, often affecting eyesight, are caused by violent shaking, kicking and beating by parents.
4 Because parents hide their deeds, many cases go unnoticed: the Royal College of Psychiatrists estimate 3,000 serious injuries and 40,000 minor injuries each year in the UK.
5 Figures from other industrialized countries are equally high. Child abuse is common amongst all 'civilized' peoples.

Points to consider

1 Information about aggressiveness towards babies is of worldwide concern. Everyone connected with child welfare must be aware of its presence.
2 The fact that child abuse occurs in the first years of life shows that crying, sleeping, and feeding problems put parents under pressures they may be unable to cope with.
3 Government policy needs to be directed at helping parents with external problems: better housing, less financial pressure, more care facilities for small children such as nurseries, playgroups, adventure playgrounds.
4 Local agencies, whether state-run or voluntary, need to offer immediate practical help such as counselling (helping the parent understand what is causing the problems), or taking control of the child while the parent has a much-needed break.

5   Parents must feel able to go for help without being ashamed. The National Society for the Prevention of Cruelty to Children (NSPCC), the health visitor, and the social worker are all trained to understand these problems.

6   Parents need to go for help early, to prevent things getting worse. There is, after all, no cure for a dead baby.

Babies have been murdered and tortured throughout recorded history; child abuse is nothing new. But what is new is the <u>understanding</u> that violent feelings towards a baby can come from any kind of parents. Naturally, they suppress these feelings. They find safe outlets for their aggressive urges in competitive sports, in tackling immense tasks like painting the house, or dancing at the disco until they are exhausted. But they suffer secret guilts and terrors, knowing these angry feelings are there in the first place. There is no need for this kind of emotional pain. <u>Feeling</u> aggressive and <u>being</u> aggressive are entirely different things. Parents who are afraid of their own aggressive feelings must go for advice and help at once. They must not take the risk of damaging their baby.

Throughout this book, emphasis has been laid on what the <u>child</u> needs to develop his full physical, mental and emotional potential. Parents are shown as wise, calm, soothing, understanding; immensely kind and loving; self-sacrificing as they put the child's needs first. Of course parents are not like this all the time. They are normal people with normal human failings. They lose their tempers, make unwise decisions, nag at the dawdling toddler, get bored with the prattle of school-children. None of this matters. Not much affects a child who is loved unconditionally. Parents need not strive to be perfect – they are, anyway, in the eyes of their small child.

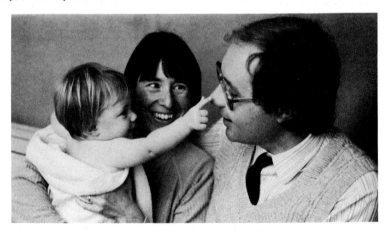

Questions

1   **Copy out the five sentences listing the damage done to babies. If you do not live in Britain, find out your country's figures and copy them out.**

2   **How can parents get rid of their aggressive urges safely?**

3   **Write a short essay, stating the reasons why it is important that parents understand aggressive feelings, and what they can do if these feelings become very powerful.**

4   **Give at least three examples of the ways in which parents could receive more help from the state.**

Further work on Chapter 7

1 Below is a list of some voluntary agencies concerned with helping children with special needs. Their addresses are in the telephone directories. Choose one agency, and either write or make a visit to their local branch. Do a full project on their work, with special reference to the way parents of disabled children benefit from belonging to such groups.

Action for the Crippled Child, Sussex
Association for Spina Bifida and Hydrocephalus, London
British Diabetic Association, London
British Epilepsy Association, London
Cystic Fibrosis Research Trust, London
The Down's Babies Association (Mongolism), Birmingham
Elizabeth Fitzroy Homes for the Handicapped, London
National Association for Deaf/Blind and Rubella Children, Birmingham
National Society for Mentally Handicapped Children, London
National Society for the Prevention of Cruelty to Children, London
National Association for the Welfare of Children in Hospital, London
National Society for Brain Damaged Children, Birmingham
Scottish Society for Mentally Handicapped Children, Glasgow
The Spastics Society, London
Sunshine Homes for Blind Children, London

2 Visit a special school in your local area and write an account of your observations of the help given to children with learning difficulties.

3 Visit your local education authority or careers office for details on the training and career prospects of nursery nurses. Give reasons why such work may, or may not, appeal to you.

4 Write to the Chartered Society of Physiotherapists, London for information on their work in hospitals and schools. Make notes on what you have learned.

5 Save the Children Fund and War on Want are two voluntary agencies concerned with overseas aid. Visit one of their local branches and write an account of the work being done.

6 Do a full project on either (a) adoption or (b) fostering. You can get further information from The Association of British Adoption & Fostering Agencies, The National Foster Care Association, the National Children's Homes, Dr Barnado's Homes.

7 What problems would the parents of a baby who is both mentally and physically handicapped have to face?
What help could they expect from external sources and how could they help their baby at home, during the first five years?   (O)

8 (a) Name two genetically inherited defects which may be diagnosed during pregnancy. Explain how the diagnosis is carried out.
  (b) Describe some of the problems faced by the family of a mentally handicapped child.   (SUJB)